Better Meetings

Everyone Wins

Cynthia M. Herr
Barbara D. Bateman

Includes **IDEA** Updates!

IEP

RESOURCES

Authors: Cynthia M. Herr, Barbara D. Bateman

Editor: Tom Kinney

Graphic Design: Sherry Pribbenow

An Attainment Publication

RESOURCES

P.O. Box 930160

Distributed By:

Program Development Associates

5620 Business Ave. Suite B
Cicero, NY 13039

www.disabilitytraining.com

1-800-543-2119

ISBN 1-57861-561-5

Table of Contents

Dedications

I would like to dedicate this book to the two greatest teachers in my life.

To my mother, Eva F. Herr: What I know and have learned about caring about and nurturing others, I first learned from my mother who loved and nurtured me as well as the many students she taught for 28 years as a first grade teacher. She was my first model of what a good, caring teacher should be.

To my coauthor, colleague, mentor, and good friend, Dr. Barbara Bateman: You taught me about special education, how to love and honor the law, and to care passionately about the rights of children with disabilities. Through your example, I learned how to be a good teacher, to hold my students to high standards, and to write clearly so that anyone can understand. I will be forever grateful for the opportunity many years ago to be your "apprentice" and to learn from one of the true giants in the field of special education. I thank you for your friendship in my life. You are a treasure to me. May we collaborate on many more projects.

Cindy

We wish to acknowledge our heartfelt appreciation to a number of individuals who contributed to the inception, preparation, and completion of this book.

We are indebted to Mary Ann Winter-Messiers who first conceived of the idea of helping parents and professionals to conduct "kinder, more gentle" IEP meetings which result in more effective, individualized programs for children with disabilities and who helped Cindy create the original outline for the book. Cindy would also like to acknowledge Mary Ann for her constant encouragement and support.

We also thank Claudia Vincent for her meticulous eye for detail and for word processing the many versions of this book. In addition, we'd like to gratefully acknowledge Tom Kinney, editor and publisher for Attainment Company, for his enthusiastic approval of our project and his very valuable editorial assistance in bringing our book to fruition. Thanks, Tom, you've been terrific to work with during this and our other projects.

Cindy Herr and Barb Bateman

Cynthia Herr

Dr. Herr is an assistant professor and Research Associate in the Department of Special Education at the University of Oregon and has been in the field of special education for 30 years. Currently, she is the program director for the Secondary Special Education Teacher Training program at the University of Oregon and has coordinated it for the past 20 years.

Dr. Herr has written and been involved in a number of federal grant projects in the area of secondary special education. She is currently the co-director of Project AIM, which trains secondary special education teachers to administer Oregon's alternate assessments, designed as alternates to required statewide tests of achievement and is director of Project PASS to train autism specialists. In addition to grant work, Dr. Herr teaches courses in the special education department including Law and Special Education.

Throughout her career, Dr. Herr has specialized in the areas of teaching students with learning disabilities and in the impact of the law on special education. Dr. Herr taught adults with learning disabilities for seven years at the community college level before beginning her career at the University of Oregon in 1985. As a consultant, she has conducted numerous workshops and made many presentations for the Oregon Association for Children and Citizens with Learning Disabilities (ACLD), the Western College Reading Association and other professional groups. She is also a certified trainer in the University of Kansas Strategies Intervention Model and has conducted in-service training for local school districts in learning strategies developed at the University of Kansas. Dr. Herr is one of the few specialists in Oregon in the area of learning disabilities assessment with adults.

In her leisure time, Dr. Herr is an avid reader of mysteries and science fiction/fantasy books and spends time with her family: A dog, a cat, and an African Grey Parrot.

Barbara Bateman

Barbara Bateman, Ph.D., J.D. is a nationally recognized expert in special education and in special education law. She has taught special education students in public schools and institutions, conducted research in learning disabilities, assessment, visual impairments, mental retardation, attitudes toward people with disabilities, and effective instruction for children with disabilities. She joined the faculty of the special education department at the University of Oregon in 1966 and while there also held visiting or summer appointments at several universities including the University of Virginia, the University of Maine and the University of Wisconsin.

She has authored over 100 professional articles, monographs, chapters and books. Dr. Bateman graduated from the University of Oregon School of Law in 1976, the year before the federal special education law (then called P.L. 94-142 and now known as IDEA) went into effect, and since then has worked in all 50 states, serving as a hearing officer, an expert witness, a consultant to attorneys and agencies, a speaker and a teacher of special education law. Presently, Dr. Bateman is a special education consultant in private practice.

When not writing, conducting in-service education for school districts, providing assistance to parents of children with disabilities, consulting with attorneys involved in IDEA legal actions, Dr. Bateman can be found traveling the world with binoculars and snorkel in search of birds, fish, and shells.

Chapter 1

Before the IEP Meeting

Introduction

The Individuals with Disabilities Education Improvement Act (IDEA '04)[1] requires that every school child with a disability have a written education plan. Parents and school personnel all go into meetings to develop individualized education programs (IEPs) saying that they want what is best for the child, yet we hear horror stories from both school personnel and parents about meetings that deteriorate into pitched battles between school personnel and parents about what the child needs, what services will be provided, and where the child will receive those services. We believe these unproductive meeting situations can be avoided and replaced with cooperative, positive, problem-solving sessions.

For parents of children who have disabilities, the IEP meeting is their primary opportunity for communication with school personnel about their child's education. For the school personnel, the IEP meeting provides an unparalleled chance to meaningfully and constructively involve the parents in planning the special services needed by the child.

For both parents and school personnel, the IEP meeting, in the words of the U.S. Office of Education, "enables [them], as equal participants, to jointly decide [1] what the child's needs are, [2] what *services* will be provided to meet those needs, and [3] what the anticipated outcomes may be" (Appendix C to IDEA Regulations, 1981).

In theory, the IEP meeting is a time when parents and school personnel, as equals, communicate openly and make decisions jointly. In too many cases, it has become a hostile encounter, filled with suspicion and ill will. In even more cases, IEP meetings are experienced by parents as a non-happening where they are passive, school personnel present a "draft" IEP, ask the parents to sign it, and then the meeting is over.

The main purpose of this book is to provide guidance to both school personnel and parents about how to communicate more clearly, more efficiently, and more compassionately with each other in order to streamline the IEP meeting process and facilitate the provision of an appropriate education to the child. When all the IEP team members focus clearly on the child and his or her educational needs, communicate as reasonable adults who have the interests of the child at heart and also have a clear understanding of what IDEA '04 does and does not require, much

---

[1] 20 U.S.C. §1400 et seq. When IDEA Regulations are cited (34 CFR Part 300), they are the 1999 Regulations. When the statute is cited, it is the IDEA '04. When we refer to IDEA without a year, it means that IDEA '04 did not change IDEA '97 and so is still good law.

can be accomplished. The single, most important goal of IDEA '04—the provision of an effective, *free, appropriate public education* (FAPE) to children with disabilities—can be met with a minimum of stress and anxiety on everyone's part.

This book does not deal with the IDEA process by which a child is determined to be eligible for IDEA special education and related services. We assume that if parents and school personnel are meeting to develop an IEP, an appropriate evaluation has been conducted and the evaluation team has determined that the child requires special education and meets the criteria for at least one of the 13 categories of disabilities detailed in IDEA. We begin with the first step in developing an IEP for a child with a disability—preparing for the meeting and gathering a legally constituted IEP team at an agreed upon time and place—and continue from there with recommendations that will result in a legally correct and educationally useful IEP for that child.

Our Primary Objectives Are:

1. To provide, in clear and understandable terms, the steps that school personnel and parents can take to create an IEP that addresses a child's unique educational needs and guarantees that child a free, appropriate education;

2. To provide suggestions and tips to school personnel and parents for participating in IEP meetings graciously and compassionately with a clearer understanding of each other's perspectives and concerns.

The Book is Divided into Three Main Sections:

1. Before the IEP meeting
2. Conducting an IEP meeting and developing a legal IEP
3. Ensuring the provision of FAPE after the meeting

We hope that the information we have provided will be understandable and useful to both parents and school personnel. A well-written IEP requires hard work and commitment on the part of all IEP members. May the suggestions offered here make the task of IEP writing less stressful and more satisfying, and may they result in a better education for all children with disabilities.

Good Communication is Key

Clear, focused, and positive communication is critical to the success of any meeting and never is that more true than in IEP meetings. Some of the benefits of good communication are apparent. The meetings are more pleasant, less stressful, more efficient, and the information flow is more accurate and efficient. Two additional benefits of good communication that may not be quite so obvious but are very important were suggested by recent experiences of the University of Michigan Health System (Tanner, 2004). For two years, the physicians practicing in that system have defied the long medical tradition of paternalism and have been giving patients complete information about treatment errors and difficulties, and offering apologies, when appropriate. Not only has this new open frankness soothed upset patients and helped maintain good relationships with them, but the doctors' attorney fees have dropped from $3 million a year to $1 million and the number of lawsuits and notices of intent to sue have dropped by 50%. In fact, Dr. Steve Kramar, then the hospital's chief of staff, said, "Not only was it the right thing to do, but over the long haul, we were saving money by doing things this way" (p. 2). One researcher found that lawsuits were more likely to result from personal anger at the doctor than from the medical error itself. There is no reason to doubt these findings also apply to special education disputes. As long as parents believe that school personnel truly value them and their child and are trying their best to serve them all well, there will be far fewer hearings or lawsuits.

Many books have been written on developing and maintaining effective communication. A few of these are listed in Figure 1.1.

Selected References on Communication

Christopher, C. (1996). Building parent-teacher communication. Lanham, MD: Rowman & Littlefield.

Kroth, R.L. (1997). Strategies for communicating with parents and families of exceptional children. Denver, CO: Love.

Lawrence-Lightfoot, S. (2003). The essential conversation: What parents and teachers can learn from each other. New York: Ballantine Books.

Lynch, E.W., & Hanson, M.J. (2004). Developing cross-cultured competence: A guide to working with children and their families (3rd ed.). Baltimore: Paul H. Brooks.

Fig. 1.1: Selected references on communication

Certain communication principles loom especially large in the context of IEP meetings. Both parents and school personnel should be open to each other's perspective, be willing to listen and truly hear, as well as to express their own views politely, succinctly, and as objectively as possible. All parties in the IEP meeting must be willing to negotiate and perhaps compromise. Major aspects of negotiation and compromise include the ability to problem solve creatively, to conceive of new solutions, and to be willing to try and then evaluate a less-than-first choice approach. Here are a few simple guidelines that IEP teams may follow to improve communication:

1. Speak to others as you would be spoken to.

2. Listen to others as you would be listened to.

3. Check to insure you understood and were understood correctly.

4. Recognize that problems have solutions. Our task is to find them.

5. Above all—remember that this meeting is about what the child needs and how we can address those needs.

In addition to all team members concentrating on the positive aspects of communication, some negatives need to be avoided by all. Interruptions, domination of the discussion, loudness, inappropriate language, extreme emotionality, anger and off-task digressions are not helpful.

As in any purposeful meeting, staying on topic is vital. All team members should center their communication around the child's needs, meeting those needs appropriately and then accurately assessing the child's progress.

Special Considerations for School Personnel

It is appropriate for the school personnel to hold a planning meeting to consider how they will structure the IEP meeting and discuss any draft proposals they wish to make. What is not acceptable in a pre-meeting is *any* decision-making about the child or about the type or amount of services to be offered. All actual decisions must be made at the IEP meeting by the full team.

"It is not permissible for an agency to have their IEP completed before the IEP meeting begins. Agency staff may come ... with prepared recommendations ..." (*Letter to Anonymous*, 41 IDELR 11 (OSEP 2003))

Many school personnel have found it useful to have a trained meeting facilitator chair IEP meetings. That person may or may not be a member of the team and may or may not be used for all IEP meetings. Especially for first IEPs and for contentious situations, a facilitator can be extremely helpful.

If the chairperson of each IEP meeting is prepared to present and structure each topic, being sure that parents are recognized as the full and equal participants they are, the meeting can move along efficiently. Having clear ground rules and structure for the meeting are basic, and a key element in maintaining good communication during the IEP meeting is that all team members have the same understanding of the topic being discussed at any moment and that all stay on that topic until it is finished. Without necessarily using a script as such, the chairperson of the IEP meeting can greatly facilitate the meeting by introducing each topic clearly, e.g. "Now we need to list Jeff's unique educational needs. First let's just brainstorm quickly, then we can discuss each proposed need. Maria, would you please list these on the easel under the heading 'Jeff needs ...'? I'll start with 'Jeff needs a quiet place to do his seatwork' and 'He needs to write more legibly.' Next?"

Special Considerations for School Personnel

☐ Hold planning meeting prior to IEP meeting to brainstorm.

☐ Use a trained meeting facilitator for initial or challenging IEP meetings.

☐ Set clear ground rules and agenda for the meeting.

☐ Chairperson of meeting should be clear about topics and keep everyone on task.

☐ Recognize parents as experts about their child.

Two preliminary considerations IDEA requires the team to deal with—strengths of the child and educational concerns of the parents—should be structured for both receptivity to parents' perceptions and for efficiency. The parents can be informed before the meeting that they will be asked to share what they see as their child's three or four major strengths pertinent to educational programming. They can also be asked to prepare to share their major concerns for their child's education. Of course, these strengths and concerns need not be written on the IEP. What does need to be indicated on the IEP is that these matters *were considered*. Similarly, the IEP team must consider recent evaluations of the child, and the academic, developmental and functional needs of the child.

Typically, school personnel develop a routine agenda for IEP meetings to ensure that all the necessary topics are covered. Ideally, these topics include the eight required elements of the IEP (see Table 1.1):

Table 1.1: Required Elements of the IEP

1. Present levels of performance (in all identified areas of unique educational needs)

2. Measurable annual goals. Short-term objectives or benchmarks are now required only for those few children who are assessed against alternate standards under No Child Left Behind (2001).

3. Statement of research-based special education, to the extent practicable, related services, supplementary aids and services and program modifications and supports for school personnel

4. Explanation of any non-participation with non-disabled children

5. Statement regarding child's participation in State or district-wide assessments

6. Starting date, frequency, location, and duration of services

7. Statement of how the child's progress toward meeting the annual goals will be measured and when periodic reports on progress will be provided to parents

8. For children 16 years old and older, measurable transition goals including measurable postsecondary goals

The order of the topics in a meeting can vary, of course, and often will. A skilled facilitator will be able to recognize that some participants do not function well in a highly structured framework and will guide the discussion so that all topics are covered. The thread of such meetings may wind round and round, but will touch all essential bases.

Finally, all school personnel should make a special effort to convey that they recognize the parents' extensive knowledge of their own child's needs, characteristics, and behaviors and that they, the school personnel, are not the "experts" on all aspects of the child's individualized program. The IEP focuses on the child as a unique individual and all IEP team members need to show a genuine interest in that child and his or her uniqueness.

Special Considerations for Parents

As indicated, school personnel are responsible for IEP meeting ground rules, for providing a logically structured and sequenced agenda, and for maintaining respect for the parents as full partners in the process. Parents, on the other hand, are responsible for asking questions, providing pertinent information, respecting the perspectives of other team members, staying on task and advocating effectively and appropriately for their child. An invaluable resource for parents who wish to become more effective advocates is **From Emotions to Advocacy** (Wright & Wright, 2001).

When parents are not fully satisfied with their understanding of something said at an IEP meeting, it is incumbent upon them to ask, and then to ask follow-up questions, if necessary. The possibility of requesting written explanatory information should also be considered. IDEA '04 does not speak to this practice directly, but it surely appears to be consistent with the law's recognition of the parents as fully informed and equal partners in the IEP process.

A major responsibility of parents is to provide information about their child to the rest of the team. In preparing for an IEP meeting, the parents need to focus on their role as "full and equal participants" who know their child better than anyone else. From their wealth of feelings and knowledge about the child and their experience with him or her, parents should choose what is most relevant to communicate to the rest of the team. The purpose of the IEP team and the reason for IEP meetings is to determine the child's unique needs and what services are appropriate to address them. All parties to the IEP process should center their communication around the child's needs and meeting them appropriately. Of course there is much more to each of us than just our needs, but the IEP focus is specifically on needs. Nevertheless, some of the child's strengths will also be pertinent to deciding what services will benefit him or her.

Parents also need to remain aware of the realities the other team members face. This is not to say parents should ever stop short of seeking a free, appropriate public education (FAPE) for their child. That never needs to happen. But at the same time, local educational agencies (LEAs) face very real limitations in personnel, money, time, and sometimes even expertise. IDEA '04 does not allow these limitations to be used as a legal defense for a failure to provide FAPE; nevertheless, the limitations are real. These limitations can motivate all parties to be open to creative solutions to service issues. Sometimes a non-traditional approach can be as effective as and far less expensive than a more common one. It is especially important that parents avoid making rigid demands for a certain amount of a particular service. It is possible, for example, that a peer friendship program (zero cost) could be just as effective as 1:1 counseling, for a particular child, in overcoming social timidity. Similarly, a rubber ball on a pencil might solve a handwriting problem as well as weeks of expensive therapy.

Children often show quite different behaviors in different settings and, therefore, school personnel may have seen behaviors different from what the parents see, and this should be respected. At the same time, school personnel should never lose sight of the fact that parents know their child far better than anyone else possibly can.

Special Considerations for Parents

✓ Ask questions

✓ Provide pertinent information about your child

✓ Respect others' perspectives

✓ Be aware of existing agency limitations (e.g., school personnel, time, financial constraints)

✓ Stay on topic during the IEP meeting

✓ Consider bringing simple snacks to the meeting

If there are genuine areas of uncertainty or disagreement about a child's behavior or other performances, it would be appropriate for parents to request any relevant evaluations be completed before the IEP meeting, so the results are available to the team.

Many IEP teams frequently fail to complete the development or review of the IEP within a reasonable time because of disagreements, digressions and tangents. Usually school personnel will set the agenda for the meeting, but it is important for parents to be able to request items to be included on the agenda, provided only that those matters are within the purview of the IEP team. Once the topics for a meeting have been clearly laid out, it is then incumbent on all team members to stay on topic. Parents should remember that the IEP is a special benefit IDEA provides to eligible children, in addition to ordinary parent-teacher or parent-principal meetings and other benefits available to all children. Decisions about the child's special education program and services must be made by the IEP team, but many other matters can be dealt with as they would be for any child. Such matters can be dealt with outside of the IEP meeting. IEP teams need to address only those matters that address a child's unique educational needs.

Not all communication is verbal. We all know that body language, posture, eye contact and other actions can convey clear and sometimes strong messages. Parents might want to consider bringing simple snacks to an IEP meeting. This is a polite and thoughtful gesture which can add a desirable positive social atmosphere and convey appreciation to school personnel. An energy boost could be a real plus for everyone especially if the meeting is early morning or late afternoon. A tiny note of caution is not to overdo the snacks or presentation in a way that would be perceived as attempting to pressure the team.

Mutual Understandings of the IEP Process

Ideally all members of the IEP team come to the first meeting with the same understanding of the fundamentals of the IEP process. The invitation the parents receive is crucial in developing this understanding. One of the most important preparatory tasks for school personnel is to insure that the invitation sets an appropriate tone and conveys the necessary information.

The Invitation Sets the Stage

The most important invitation[2] ever to an IEP meeting is the first such invitation the parents receive. The next most important invitation is the first that they receive from a new (to them) school. The invitation can initiate a positive, cooperative, and legally correct IEP process in which parents are respected as full and equal participants.

When a child has been found IDEA-eligible, the next step is the IEP meeting. For some parents this will be the first encounter they have with the IEP process. For other parents, the first IEP will mark the transition away from early intervention services and the Individualized Family Service Plan (IFSP) their child and the family had during his or her preschool years. In either case, it is crucial that the IEP—the document and its development—be fully explained to the parents.

For parents who have no particular expectations and no previous familiarity with the IFSP process, the invitation to the first IEP meeting can be very straight forward. The key elements are that the invitation sets a positive tone and includes all the information required by IDEA. Figure 1.2 shows a sample IEP meeting invitation.

Smoothing the Transition from IFSP to IEP

The IFSP process includes a major focus on the *family's* resources, priorities, concerns, outcomes to be achieved, and needed services. Parents familiar with the IFSP process may be surprised and disappointed to find the family is not an explicit focus of the IEP. They should be forewarned and prepared. Without proper preparation, the first IEP meeting may make the parents feel they have been denied "rights" to which they are entitled. This is not the case, but how are parents to know the difference between an IFSP and IEP if they are not informed? No one wants the first IEP meeting (or any IEP meeting) to conclude with a loss of trust and/or breakdown in open communication. Yet this is exactly what may happen unless early intervention and school personnel help parents understand the differences between the IFSP and IEP processes and entitlements. IDEA '04 recommends, in order to avoid this situation, that parents request that the LEA invite the IFSP provider to attend the initial IEP meeting:

In the case of a child who was previously served under part C [early intervention services], an invitation to the initial IEP meeting shall, at the request of the parent, be sent to the part C Service Coordinator or other representatives of the part C system to assist with the smooth transition of services. (20 U.S.C. §1414(d)(1)(D))

---

[2] The invitation to an IEP meeting is just that—an invitation. It is not a "prior written notice" although this fact is lost on many local education agencies (LEAs).

Dear Mr. and Mrs. Atsushi,

As part of the evaluation team, you know that we recently determined that your daughter Mihoko is eligible for an Individualized Education Program (IEP) to meet her special academic, social, behavioral, physical, and other needs. She is now legally entitled to (1) special education, which is specially designed instruction to meet those unique needs; (2) related services such as transportation or physical therapy, which may be necessary to enable her to benefit from her special education; and (3) any necessary services, aids, modifications, or accommodations if and when she is in regular education classes, including support for the personnel working with her.

We need to have a meeting to plan Mihoko's IEP. At this meeting we will discuss your concerns about her education, her strengths, her unique characteristics and needs, the services appropriate to address these, and the ways we should judge how well the services are helping Mihoko to make progress at school. You are a full and equal partner with the school personnel in deciding what will be included in Mihoko's IEP. The enclosed sample IEP for a fictional child will give you an idea of what kinds of things an IEP might include. Please give some thought to these matters ahead of time, so we can exchange ideas at the meeting.

You are welcome to bring anyone you wish who is knowledgeable about your child to the meeting. Some parent groups (e.g., Learning Disabilities Association, Association for Retarded Citizens) have advocates available to attend IEP meetings with parents. You may choose to have Mihoko present for all or part of the meeting. It is often useful for the child to participate, and she may feel more involved with and committed to her IEP goals if she does so. If you decide Mihoko won't be at the meeting, please consider bringing a picture of her to remind us all that the only purpose of the meeting is to plan an educational program just for her. Stan Jones, who helped evaluate Mihoko, and Cara Evans, her regular classroom teacher, will be at this first IEP meeting. The principal, Edneisha Oakes, will attend the IEP meeting as the LEA representative, and I will be there as Mihoko's special education teacher, and I will explain the evaluation, if questions arise.

We have tentatively scheduled this meeting for Feb. 2 at 3:00 PM here at Caesar Chavez Elementary School. If this is not convenient, please call and we will arrange another time. In addition to the sample IEP, I have enclosed a brochure explaining your legal rights. Please look it over. If you have any questions, we can discuss them at the meeting.

Sincerely,

Andrea Harrison

Andrea Harrison

Special Education Teacher

Fig. 1.2: Sample IEP Meeting Invitation

Mutually Agreed Upon Time and Place for the IEP Meeting

Parents sometimes wonder about the extent to which the school personnel must go to find a mutually agreed upon time and place for an IEP meeting. IDEA does not define what 'mutually agreed upon' means. However, in comments to the regulatory requirement, the U.S. Department of Education said the key factor in the regulation (34 C.F.R. §300.345(a)) is "that public agencies effectively communicate with parents about the up-coming IEP meeting, and *attempt to arrange a mutually agreed upon time and place for the meeting*. This process should accommodate the parents' work schedules to ensure that one or both parents are afforded the opportunity to participate" (Fed. Reg. Vol. 64, No. 48 at 12587).

This opportunity to participate is central. All parties should remember that, if necessary, participation may be by telephone, e-mail, fax, or other methods. While there are obvious advantages to having all team members physically present, other arrangements can also be satisfactory. IDEA '04 provides that a team member may be excused from attendance at an IEP meeting if the parent and local education agency (LEA) agree. However, if the meeting deals with that member's area of special knowledge or expertise, then the excused member must give his or her written input to the school and the parents prior to the meeting.

Support for the Parents

Another aspect of the mutual understanding of IDEA and the IEP process that is important for all to share is a knowledge of the support available to parents. IDEA is designed so that parents have a great deal of responsibility for insuring the law is implemented properly. In fact, as far as obtaining the promised free and appropriate education for an individual child, the power to make it happen is vested in parents. When parents are unaware of their IDEA rights and/or IDEA provisions for resolving disputes, the law does not operate properly and children are the likely losers.

Parent Rights Information

The main vehicle school personnel use to inform parents about their IDEA rights and procedural protections is a brochure commonly called something like "Parent Rights." Some local education agencies (LEAs) prepare their own brochure; others use a state-provided version. These brochures range in completeness, accuracy, understandability, and even legibility from excellent to very poor. Regardless of the quality of the information and its presentation, the reality is that many parents do not fully use these "Parent Rights" brochures. The rights statements are sometimes regarded much like insurance policies—filed to be read (or not) when a problem arises.

IDEA '04 critics have noted that placing responsibility on LEAs for dissemination of parent rights information may not have been ideal. To some extent, parent groups and advocacy organizations have also filled this role of rights dissemination. However, the number of parents involved in the IEP process who are in contact with these groups is limited and sometimes a serious legal error may be made by a parent prior to contact with such groups. A common problem, for example, is that many parents are unaware that in a dispute over FAPE they may forfeit their right to reimbursement if they remove their child to a private placement without giving prior notice to the LEA of their intent and concerns (34 C.F.R. §300.403(d)).

"The [IDEA '04] provides that reimbursement [for private school] may be denied or reduced if the parents do not give the school district notice of their intent to remove their child from public school before they do so." (Greenland Sch. Dist. v. Amy N., 358 F. 3d 150, 40 IDELR, 203 (1st Cir. 2004))

Other errors often occur around obtaining reimbursement for independent evaluations. There is no substitute for parental knowledge of IDEA and of the rights and protections it provides.

Full and Equal Participation

No IDEA parent right is more important than that of participating as a "full and equal partner" in the IEP process. A very knowledgeable parent recently reported an incident from her child's IEP meeting. The special education teacher and parent were working on rewriting the school's "draft" goals and objectives so that they were measurable (at the parent's insistence). The parent was far more knowledgeable and skilled than the teacher who finally blurted out to the parent "Are you going to tell me how to do my job?" How revealing. Some school personnel think of developing the IEP as their responsibility, not as a joint undertaking.

> *"... No one person is responsible for or entitled to develop the IEP [including] the goals and objectives ... The entire team is charged with making these decisions." (Letter to Anonymous, 41 IDELR 11 (OSEP 2003))*

In fact, parents and LEAs are equal participants in the IEP process. However, when a dispute arises over what constitutes FAPE, the LEA has the "ultimate responsibility to ensure that the IEP includes the services that the child needs in order to receive FAPE" (34 C.F.R. Part 300, App. A at question 9), as is discussed later.

Several factors can mitigate against full parent participation. The first clearly is that parents may have no idea they are entitled to an equal role. Another is that parents may be intimidated by large numbers of school personnel, especially if titles, degrees, or other credentials are flaunted or if many personnel are not known by the parents.

> *"... [P]rocedural inadequacies that result in the loss of educational opportunity [for the child], or seriously infringe on the parents' opportunity to participate in the IEP formulation process, clearly result in the denial of a FAPE." (W.G. v. Bd. of Trustees, 960 F. 2d 1470, 42 IDELR 57 (9th Cir. 1992))*

In too many LEAs it is routine to have 15 or 20 school personnel attend IEP meetings. At the other extreme, some teams have only a special education teacher and parent, perhaps with an administrator who steps in to greet the parent briefly. Three or four carefully selected school personnel (e.g., special education and regular education teachers who know the child, a school psychologist, and an LEA representative) can usually both fulfill the legal requirements and carry out the special education tasks that go into developing an appropriate IEP.

Sometimes a friend, an advocate, or an attorney can support a parent's participation in an IEP meeting. Their presence can also change the atmosphere and dynamics of the meeting, sometimes in a desirable way, but not always.

It could be most helpful and productive if every LEA shared a video-tape of a well-conducted, positive, and successful IEP meeting with all school personnel and with parents anticipating their first meeting. Many IEP team members have never seen a well-handled meeting.

Diversity Considerations

Bridging cultural differences in IEP meetings can be challenging for school personnel. It can also be extremely rewarding and more than worth the efforts. For example, some parents may be fearful of participating in a meeting with school (government) authorities, others may not initially understand that the meeting is about benefits for their child, not punishments, or some parents may need an interpreter in order to understand the IEP proceeding. In some cultural groups, certain IEP topics such as transition, might be meaningless for a daughter whose after school life is predetermined and not open to discussion. There may be important considerations as to which member of the family or the extended family is the appropriate person to speak to or about certain matters.

It is incumbent on the school personnel to learn how to put all parents at ease and to avoid cultural blunders that could undermine the IEP process and future relations with families.

When the LEA is ethnically or culturally diverse, school personnel should work to establish close ties with members of the minority community who can serve as liaisons and possibly interpreters at IEP meetings.

IDEA also requires that LEAs shall "take whatever action is necessary to ensure that the parent understands the proceeding at the IEP meeting, including arranging for an interpreter for parents with deafness or whose native language is other than English" (34 C.F.R. §300 345(e)). Individual leaders within a city's various cultural communities may be able to assist school personnel in contacting individuals who may be qualified to act as interpreters at IEP meetings. Churches and other community agencies may also provide referrals to individuals who will agree to interpret at an IEP meeting.

In general, school personnel should avoid asking a family member to interpret for his or her family at an IEP meeting as this may cause a cultural or emotional conflict for that family member.

What an IEP is and is Not

A mutual understanding of what is and is not part of an IEP can contribute significantly to the efficiency and pleasantness of an IEP meeting. A recent review of a child's file revealed that the parents had insisted the school personnel include in the IEP section on present levels of performance over 14 pages summarizing 24 independent evaluations! At the same time, all 24 of the evaluations, in their entirety, were in the child's school education records. No need nor purpose is served by cluttering IEPs with information readily available elsewhere. A two hour long "IEP meeting" was spent arguing over whether the 14 pages of evaluation data would be included in the IEP. Nothing was accomplished and another meeting had to be scheduled. What a waste of everyone's time and energy. IDEA '04 is emphatic that nothing beyond the federal requirements need be included in the IEP (20 U.S.C. §1414 (d)(i)(A)(ii)).

Federal education agencies have repeatedly said that the IDEA requirements for an IEP can be met in 3-5 pages in almost all cases. This alone makes it painfully clear that most IEPs contain far more than is required. If all team members understand exactly what IDEA requires be on the IEP, the meeting can proceed smoothly. If a state or an LEA mandates additional information to be included, beyond what IDEA requires, that is also good for all to know.

Parents sometimes feel that having particular information included in the IEP is the best way to insure it will be noted or acted upon. While there may be some truth to this, there may be other ways, such as discussing the information (especially if the meeting is being taped) or including it in the child's file.

Perhaps the biggest misconception about IEPs is that they must include the child's entire education program. This is not true. The IEP is a special education document which should deal with the individualized aspects of the child's education. After all, it is an Individualized Education Program. The regular education part of a child's program need not be dealt with in the IEP except for a statement of "How the child's disability affects the child's involvement and progress in the general education curriculum" (20 U.S.C. §1414 (d)(1)(A)(i)(I)(aa)).

In this day of standards, tests, and "accountability," it is understandable that people are concerned about all children's progress in the regular curriculum. However, to require busy teachers to select and copy portions of the regular curriculum onto the IEP is clearly nonsensical. Yet it happens frequently. It is critically important to include in the IEP the special services and accommodations that are *necessary to enable* the child to participate and progress in the regular curriculum, just as IDEA '04 requires (20 U.S.C. §1414 (d)(1)(A)(i)(IV)(bb)). That is not the same as including the curriculum itself or even parts of it.

Understanding Others' Perspectives

One of the most helpful things IEP team members can do before the meeting is to reflect on the perspectives of the rest of the team—to walk in their shoes for a few moments.

The LEA's Perspective

Each LEA is unique and by no means do all LEAs have a shared perspective about IEP meetings. In many LEAs IEP meetings are positive, pleasant, relaxed, and focused on providing services children need. However, in a few LEAs IEP meetings are hostile, very brief, and designed to offer as little as possible to a child, regardless of the law. This description sounds harsh, but sadly it is no exaggeration.

Nor do all school personnel within an LEA share the same perspective of IEP meetings; however, some constants do exist. The first of these universals is concern about time. IDEA is clear that we, as a society, are committed to making a FAPE available to every child who has a disability. Part of what is required to do that, obviously, is time. On average, about 10% of a school's population is IDEA-eligible. Time is required for the full and individualized evaluations and re-evaluations of each of those children, for progress assessments, for report writing, and for eligibility meetings. In addition, IEP meetings require substantial school personnel time to manage the logistics of having the right people in the right room at the appointed time, and to prepare for and hold the meeting. All of this precedes the major time investment—the actual provision of the intensive, individualized special instruction and related services a child needs and the law requires. If we add to this the fact that most LEAs struggle constantly with special education personnel shortages and high turnover, we begin to appreciate that time can be a real problem.

And beyond all this is the paperwork burden which has been so heavy it has driven many excellent people out of special education altogether.

School personnel can hardly be blamed for hoping each IEP team efficiently concludes its necessary business and for dreading difficult situations that result in multiple, often unpleasant, IEP meetings with little accomplished. When the IEP team is deliberating about actual services to be provided, time concerns loom large. Suppose the special education teacher on the team has been told that only one half-time aide will be available for the self-contained classroom, and the IEP team's discussion moves on to the child's need for a 1:1 aide at all times. It is easy to stand apart and say that if the aide is necessary for that child to receive FAPE, the LEA must provide it. Often, however, it is not that clear. From the LEA perspective, the child may need an aide available when necessary, but should not be stigmatized or made dependent by having the aide constantly present. Just as the parents should advocate for what they believe the child needs, so should the school personnel.

Another factor that sometimes affects school personnel who are team members is their less than total certainty about what the law actually requires in a particular situation. This can be exacerbated by the presence of a very knowledgeable parent or parent advocate. If the parents bring an attorney (or sometimes an advocate) to an IEP meeting, many LEA personnel will refuse to hold the meeting until their attorney can be present. This results in a cancelled meeting and is not conducive to smooth relationships in the next scheduled meeting.

Another LEA perspective that can occasionally interfere in an IEP meeting is a feeling on the part of some personnel that no matter what they offer, what services they provide, it won't be enough to satisfy the parent. In a recent situation, for example, the parents had been frustrated for years over what they saw as inadequate progress of their daughter with autism. As a ten year old she was functioning much like a six year old, academically, socially, and linguistically. School personnel felt they had done a good job, that the girl was progressing very appropriately, and that the parents were unreasonably demanding and ungrateful. During a reevaluation, school personnel learned that the parents had always believed the girl had average intelligence, when in fact all her evaluations (over a 6-year period in the same LEA) indicated her ability level was below the 1st percentile. This sad misperception on the parents' part speaks to a common problem created by our use of euphemisms and technical terms which can obscure the real nature of some aspects of disability and create impossible expectations.

Clearly there are many other reasons school personnel might feel their efforts are unappreciated, but differences between their expectations for the child and those of the parents can too often be a factor. Whatever the cause, one result of feeling unappreciated may be to give less effort than otherwise.

Another factor that influences school personnel perspectives on IEP meetings is the ever present reality of LEA protocol, channels and hierarchies. Some staff even believe they dare not advocate for any evaluations, services, or placements that would necessitate increased LEA expenditures. An itinerant special education teacher in a large urban LEA was recently awarded just under a million dollars in damages[3] for the retaliation (including non-renewal) she experienced in her LEA for her outspoken advocacy on behalf of her special education students. The processes by which school personnel become fearful of the consequences of advocacy are not always easily uncovered, but that fear can nevertheless be very real. By far the most difficult question a professor of special education law faces in every class comes from a conscientious student-LEA employee who asks, "What should I do if I've been told not to suggest any service we don't already have, not to offer more of any service than our standard amount, or not to recommend a placement other than mainstream general education?"

> *Some staff even believe they dare not advocate for any evaluations, services, or placements that would necessitate increased LEA expenditures.*

The Parents' Perspective

Especially at the all-important first IEP meeting, parents may have little idea of what to expect or what the expectations are for their participation. It is up to the school personnel to make available appropriate orientation information. At a minimum, the first IEP meeting invitation should provide information about parent groups and advocacy groups that the parent might contact. Many later misunderstandings can be avoided by providing clear and complete information in an understandable and appealing way on this first opportunity.

When parents understand their child is entitled to what FAPE entails, they frequently become the child's leading advocate. They know their child's needs and problems from the inside out and naturally focus on how to address their child's problems rather than on problems facing school personnel.

---

[3] *Settlegoode v. Portland Pub.* Schs., 371 F.3d 503 (9th Cir. 2004).

Being the parent of a child with a disability, a child who probably doesn't perform in school as others do, is not easy. It's common for parents to experience more than their share of frustration and to feel misunderstood. It's important for school personnel to acknowledge that they recognize parents as the true experts on their child and as vital team members who are full and equal participants in the problem solving process that is IEP development. If, at the first meeting, the parents are presented with a completed or nearly completed IEP, neatly typed, even if it has the word "DRAFT" on it, they are not likely to believe they are truly equal team members. Instead of using a condescending, patronizing, and 'borderline legal' draft IEP, how much better if parents and school personnel all prepare informal one-page charts where they list (a) what they see as the child's most important educational needs, (b) a couple of possible ways to address those needs, and perhaps (c) a reasonable goal in each area of need. A quick comparison of these charts at the beginning of the meeting could provide invaluable information for the team as to what needs to be dealt with in the meeting and on the starting perspectives of both parent and school personnel. It goes without saying that such charts must be treated with total respect. Not all charted items will necessarily be included in the final IEP, but they nevertheless are valuable.

Parents will naturally be interested in the relationship each of the team members has with their child and introductions should center on this and especially on how well that person knows the child. Parents may well want to share more information about themselves than that they are parents. If a parent, for example, is also a teacher, psychologist, child care specialist, attorney, pediatrician, software specialist, audiologist, linguist, or any of many other possibilities, that expertise is important to the team. If the parent is a single dad working two jobs, that may also be important for the team to know.

The overriding fact of parents' perspectives is that they want their child to function in the highest, fullest, happiest ways possible, and they want the entire team to be centered on providing a FAPE to their child, truly individualized to meet his or her needs. If parents perceive that needed services are being deliberately withheld, they cannot react well. On the other hand, as long as the entire team conveys genuine interest in meeting the child's needs and fulfilling IDEA's expectations and entitlements, almost all parents will cooperate to the best of their ability.

Preparing for the Meeting

All IEP team members have certain responsibilities for preparing for an IEP meeting. School personnel must invite parents to the meeting, make arrangements for the location, ensure that all relevant individuals attend (unless parents agree otherwise), and provide the most recent, pertinent evaluation information. School personnel must also be aware of their LEA's position on taping IEP meetings in case parents ask.

Parents, on the other hand, have the responsibility to decide who will attend the meeting-both or only one of them, their child, and any other individual who is knowledgeable about the child. Parents must also decide if they feel the need to invite an advocate or attorney to the meeting. Parents have the responsibility to provide relevant information about their child and the child's particular disability as well as to prepare what they want to say and present at the meeting.

School Personnel's Preparations

The LEA has certain powers and responsibilities for the convening and conduct of all IEP meetings. However, some of these loom larger for the first meeting for a family or for a meeting that the LEA anticipates may be challenging.

The Invitation

The invitation to the IEP meeting must be given early enough that the parents can arrange to attend the meeting at a mutually agreed upon time and place. The invitation must state who will be at the meeting and inform parents that they may bring to the meeting any individuals who have special knowledge about the child.[4]

An issue that can arise, after the first meeting, is whether and when to hold additional meetings. In the worst of circumstances, one IEP can require 10 to 20 IEP meetings (each one up to two hours or more) and still not be successfully completed.[5] In these cases, the LEA is driven to have more and more meetings because of its legal mandate to have a completed IEP in place the beginning of each school year and to have an offer of FAPE "on the table" at all times. This situation

---

[4] This is explained (34 C.F.R. §300.344 (c)) to mean the party who invites someone determines that the invitee has "knowledge or expertise." Thus it is not a limitation on who may be invited.

[5] A misunderstanding or abuse of the IEP process, but it happens far more frequently than we would think or wish.

arises most often because the LEA fails to understand its responsibility to 'toss the ball into the parents' court,' that is, to offer what it, the LEA, believes is FAPE, implement it after giving at least 10 days notice to the parents and leave it to the parents to pursue mediation, a hearing or a complaint if they disagree.

The Physical Setting

IDEA '04 appears to anticipate that some IEP meetings might be held at the parents' home in the evening or at the community center on the weekend. The reality, of course, is that they are generally held at the school, usually before or after school, on a "teacher or parent conference" day, in mid-afternoon or mid-morning when substitutes are available, or when "team teaching" is scheduled and one teacher can be spared. As taxpayers, and we all are, we appreciate this reality. However, on rare occasions, it may be the better course for school personnel to make even greater efforts to accommodate parent needs or schedules.

Whenever the meeting is held, school personnel should make every effort to insure an adequately equipped, pleasant and private setting. Years ago a memorable IEP meeting was held in an elementary school gym-cafeteria. The ten participants sat at a tiny cafeteria table with low benches, four jammed on each side and one at each end. It was summer, incredibly hot (no AC), and two janitors noisily worked nearby, often walking back and forth next to the table. The father was 6'4" tall and sat with his chin all but on his knees for the entire meeting. No refreshments, not even water, were available. The only amenity was an antique portable chalk board and a half piece of chalk. Needless to say, the only positive outcome was a clear picture of how not to hold an IEP meeting.

Attendance of Relevant School Personnel

The LEA is responsible for ensuring that all the legally required team members are included or excused by written agreement between parents and the LEA. The team is comprised of the parents, the child's regular education teacher and special education teacher, the LEA representative and someone who can interpret the instructional implications of evaluation results.

"An IEP which was prepared by [an IEP team] that lacked each of its required members is a nullity." (Bd. of Ed. of the Avon Central Sch. Div., 40 IDELR 57 (NY SEA 2003).

However, a member of the IEP team is not required to attend an IEP meeting, in whole or in part, if the parent of a child with a disability and the LEA agree in writing that the attendance of such member is not necessary because the member's area of the curriculum or related services is not being modified or discussed in the meeting. If the meeting involves the member's area of the curriculum, his or her written input is essential (20 U.S.C. §1414 (d)(1)(C)). If the child is attending a private school, someone from that school should also be there. Some private schools choose not to participate, but their input, perhaps written, is still essential.

"We reasoned that the failure to include 'the [private school] teachers most knowledgeable about [the child's] special educational levels and needs' was a violation of IDEA." (Shapiro v. Paradise Valley Unified Sch. Dist., 37 F. 3d 1072 (9th Cir. 2003))

Evaluation Information

Parents have the right to inspect and review all their child's education records and to participate in all decision-making meetings regarding the identification, evaluation, program (FAPE), and placement of their child. The IEP meeting is the forum for dealing with a child's program. Some evaluation data can be helpful in specifying present levels of performance, but for this purpose evaluation data must be very recent, very specific, and stated in terms that lead to short-term progress assessment (e.g., words read per minute, % of long division problems solved correctly, length of spontaneous utterances). Other evaluation information properly belongs in eligibility discussions or in a meeting between a parent and an evaluator who can answer parent questions or concerns.

IDEA does require that the IEP team "consider the results of the initial or most recent evaluations." Many have interpreted this to mean every available evaluation report is to be read aloud verbatim, in its entirety, at the meeting. A better view, we believe, is that all evaluation reports be made available to interested/entitled parties prior to the meeting and that at the meeting the appropriate team member (the one who "can interpret the instructional implications of evaluation results") (34 C.F.R. §300.344 (a)(5)) give a very brief statement, in ordinary language, of the important instructional implications of the evaluation data to be dealt with in the IEP. Time spent preparing such a statement would be well spent.

The amount of time now commonly spent presenting evaluation data in IEP meetings far exceeds its value and represents an astronomical waste of resources. If every IDEA child had but one IEP meeting per year (it averages substantially above that), if only 20 minutes per meeting were spent on formal evaluation data and reports, and if an average of only 5 people attended each meeting, that would represent 10 million person hours per year spent listening to percentiles, scale scores, composite scores and standard scores. Surely this time can better be spent in providing services to children.

Taping the Meeting

The state and/or LEA have the option to require, prohibit, limit or otherwise regulate the use of recording devices at IEP meetings. However, if the LEA has a policy limiting taping, it must allow exceptions when they are needed to ensure that a parent understands the IEP or the IEP process or to implement other parental rights (34 C.F.R. Part 300, App. A at question 21).

If parents wish to tape an IEP meeting, school personnel must know what the LEA's policy is and how to respond to the parents' request. An LEA policy must be written, so it is appropriate for parents to ask to see it. Sometimes people confuse local practices or custom with policy, which must be officially established by the school board in a public meeting and is written. If there is a written policy and it appears to prevent taping, school personnel must be prepared to decide if the parents' situation fits the exceptions the policy is required to provide. If parents are allowed to tape the IEP meeting, school personnel may also want to tape it.

One might wonder about the advantages and disadvantages of taping a meeting. Two possible disadvantages are readily overcome. First, some team members may initially feel intimidated and be reluctant to participate fully, but they will probably quickly become accustomed to the process. A second possible drawback to taping can occur if the person doing the taping isn't familiar with the equipment and has to disrupt the flow of the meeting to deal with it. A combination of preparation and back-up equipment eliminates this problem.

A very positive effect of taping has been observed—an increase in the level of politeness all around and a marked decrease in inappropriate and misleading LEA statements such as "We would like to provide a tutor for this child, but we can't afford it;" "The only way we could provide therapy would be if the child were labeled emotionally disturbed;" "We don't ever provide after-school tutoring;" "We require a 22 point discrepancy between WISC Full Scale IQ and the Woodcock Johnson Broad Reading Score but this child has only a 21 point discrepancy, so he is not IDEA eligible;" or "He will be subject to the School Discipline Code regardless of the IEP." Another obvious advantage to taping is that of having a complete and accurate record of the meeting, rather than the typical selective and subjective information contained in minutes or other notes.

> "... [A]n SEA or public agency has the option to require, prohibit, limit, or otherwise regulate the use of recording devices at IEP meetings ... [but] must provide for exceptions if they are necessary to ensure [parental rights]." (Letter to Anon., 40 IDELR 70 (OSEP, 2003))

If school personnel record an IEP meeting and keep the tape, then that tape is an "education record" under the Family Education Rights and Privacy Act (FERPA) and must be treated by the LEA like any other education record. On the other hand, a tape made and kept by the parent has no such protections or restrictions, as it is not covered by FERPA. The parents may do with the tape as they wish.

Parents' Preparations

Parents may have several concerns as they prepare for an IEP meeting. One of the first may be about which parent should attend, followed by what information to present to the team about their child and his or her disability. Closely related to this is planning what to say and bring to the rest of the team. Parents must also decide whether to bring an advocate, an attorney, or any other person to the meeting.

Deciding Who Will Attend

If both parents can attend the IEP meeting, that may be the best of all worlds. However, the logistics of child care, work, and transportation often prevent that. One parent may be highly emotional or prone to expressions of frustration that could be nonproductive in the meeting. Or perhaps one parent might need to listen to a tape of the meeting, replay parts, and stop it for discussion with the attending spouse, in order to fully process what transpired at the meeting. The decision about which parent, or both, will attend is left to the parents. When parents are divorced or separated, both parents must be invited unless written legal documentation has been submitted to the LEA which limits the right of one parent to participate in educational decision making.

Whether the child attends the IEP meeting is entirely up to the parent, except that when the child reaches age 16, school personnel are required to *invite* the child to the IEP meeting if transition needs or services are to be discussed (34 C.F.R. §300.344(b)). In deciding whether the child should attend, the parents may wish to consider the sensitivity of the topics that may come up, that is, how difficult it would be for the child to hear, and the ability of the child to understand and participate in the IEP development. Perhaps having the child attend a portion of the meeting could accomplish the positives of having input and some 'ownership' without the negatives of boredom or embarrassment.

Whether to bring a friend or relative for support in the meeting is entirely up to the parent and should be decided on the basis of the comfort level that such support would bring against any negatives that might accrue. The first question parents should ask themselves about hiring an attorney or advocate is whether they need one. The answer, of course, is that 'it all depends.' It depends on the nature of the problem, the parents' ease of accessing legal information through sources such as www.wrightslaw.com,[6] their contacts with knowledgeable parent support groups, their financial situation, the availability of trained advocates and the attorney's experience in special education law, to mention a few of the factors to be weighed.

If parents bring an advocate or attorney, the tone of the meeting may change for the worse. For example, school personnel may be more cautious, restrained, hesitant, hostile, grudging or suspicious. To some extent this reaction depends on the reputation of the individual advocate or attorney and the LEA's prior experience with him or her, as well as the advocate or attorney's skills. Sadly enough, some advocates

---

[6] We highly recommend this website to all parents and professionals concerned with special education.

have garnered a reputation for unreasonableness, shrillness, negativity and tactics that result in LEAs going into a defensive mode and red alert when those advocates appear. Parents are well advised to get as much objective information as they can about an advocate or attorney's reputation among LEA personnel. Of course, sometimes parents need the strongest, most aggressive assistance possible, but it is important for parents to be aware of this style and manner and of the possible consequences of enlisting such assistance. Of course, in many communities there are no options. In these situations, statewide or national parent groups and advocacy groups[7] can be very helpful.

Preparing Information About the Child

School personnel need to know the child from his or her parents' perspectives. School personnel may have ample experience with, and information about, the child's disability itself, or they may have next to none. Before parents begin to prepare information for the IEP team about their child's disability, they must be sure that it is appropriate to do so. If the child has a disability which is well known to the school personnel and with which they deal daily, then parents should concentrate on sharing the ways in which their child's needs and behaviors are not typical, given the disability. For instance, the fidgety behavior and lack of concentration shown by a 12-year old boy who has ADHD will hardly surprise a sixth grade teacher who has 32 years of experience with over a thousand 12-year old children. However, if parents can provide the information that earphones and white noise calm their son and greatly aid his concentration, that information would be relevant and helpful, as it's unique to the child.

There are also disabilities that are infrequent and may be relatively unfamiliar to school personnel, even special educators. Parents have a major head start in knowing about their child's disability. If parents believe school personnel may not know about the child's disability, first they should check this perception. For example, in many schools Asperger's Syndrome (an Autism Spectrum Disorder) is now a frustratingly common diagnosis. In other schools, it has yet to be recognized. Similarly, Williams Syndrome has become well known in a few LEAs, while other LEAs have not yet had any experience with it. Some conditions such as Treacher Collins Syndrome are so rare that few school personnel have had any experience with children who have it.

---

[7] Each state has a 'Protection and Advocacy for the Disabled' agency, often called a P & A. The name may vary, but any disabilities group can provide information about it.

If school personnel have not had experience with a child's disability, then it is fully appropriate for parents to provide helpful sources of information. A good general rule is to prepare a *one-page* resource for the LEA. Perhaps it will become evident later that additional information would be helpful and welcome. Initially, parents can help by providing a listing of the educationally relevant characteristics of the disability which their child shares. Parents might wish to list the URL for a website or two they have found especially useful. While less is better, if previous evaluations contain three or four particularly helpful observations of a child, including brief quotes (no more than one or two sentences each) from such reports identifying the dates and the names of professionals quoted, will also be appreciated. Finally, parents can offer to provide additional information and perhaps give the title and author of a *brief* article (no more than a few pages) that they have found especially pertinent and would like to share. At all times parents should remember that school personnel need and want information that relates to how and what to *teach*. Medical and other aspects of the disability are vital to parents and others working with the child, but if these have little bearing on the school's relationship to the child, they should be given a low priority.

One of the most important sources of information for the team is the child herself or himself. Prior to an IEP meeting, parents should discuss with their child, if possible and appropriate, what his or her concerns are about school, what is going well, what he or she would like to have different, what he or she thinks about his or her program, placement, peers, classes, teachers, schedule, and so on. Parents are in a superb position to filter, translate and transmit this information to the team if the child is not going to participate in the meeting.

When the child reaches the age of 16, the LEA will invite him or her to participate in the discussion of transition (to life after secondary school). At that time, she or he may speak for herself or himself, but parent input is still totally welcome and appropriate.

After school personnel begin to work with a child, additional questions may arise and parents should, of course, help provide answers. Parents and school personnel have a joint responsibility to find and share all the available information that relates to providing a free, appropriate public education to the child.

A pertinent change to the IDEA regulations in 1999 was the addition of "personnel support" as a named service that may be included in a child's IEP. When the IEP team recognizes that the school personnel working with a particular child lack background/experience with the disability involved, it is now appropriate to include necessary in-service training for school personnel in the IEP.

Planning What to Say and Bring to the Meeting

If we may begin at the end, the bottom line is that parents going into an IEP meeting should be prepared to share with the IEP team a one or two (at the most) page chart, diagram, or listing of:

1. The child's strengths;

2. The child's unique education needs;

3. Possible ways of addressing the needs; and

4. Possible performance goals for each area of need.

The listing or chart may also address (a) concerns the parents have about their child's educational experience, and (b) any questions they have about the child's identification, evaluation, program or placement. Parents should, however, recall that the IEP team's proper focus is on the child's needs and the appropriate services to address those needs. Some other issues can better be dealt with outside the IEP process.

The key to effective parent presentations to the IEP team includes a "do" and a "don't." The "do" is to be *clear and brief* about what parents believe are the three or four most important educational needs of their child. These may include behaviors (performances) that need to be increased or decreased; for example, Jake needs to read more fluently, express his ideas in writing more easily, behave better in class, show better anger management skills or have more legible handwriting. They may also include needed conditions for learning, such as a study environment free from auditory distractions, clear rules and consequences, a quiet study area, small group instruction for the presentation of new materials, or a 1:1 check to see if the child understands oral instructions given to the whole group. These "unique educational needs" (UENs) are the foundation and the focus of a child's IEP. With them clearly before the team, members can focus on how to meet these needs and how to measure a child's progress toward goals in these areas. Without this focus, one danger is that the IEP meeting can degenerate into a routine offering of minimal, readily available services, with too little attention to the critical fit between a child's needs and services.

Here are two examples of real children's needs prepared from an examination of evaluation data in their files:

Anne is a ten-year old girl who has mild to moderate autism. She needs:

1. To keep her attention and concentration focused for longer periods of time,

2. to get along better with peers and develop a real friendship,

3. to better comprehend what she reads, and

4. to increase both her speaking and listening vocabulary.

Sammy is a nine-year old fourth grader who has been diagnosed as having generalized anxiety disorder with depression and learning disabilities. His intelligence is above average. He needs:

1. To feel better about going to school (he is embarrassed by his low academics, he wants to stay home, and he is afraid to try difficult work),

2. more time to complete written work than the other children, but he shouldn't be kept in at recess to do this, and

3. a positive behavior management plan to replace the negative one in place now because now when Sammy is punished and humiliated due to his slow processing, he shuts down and performs even less well.

Other members of the team may see additional needs or ways to combine the child's needs. Parents' lists are a very important part of the needs identification process, but just part of it. Parents have every right and perhaps even an obligation to expect that the team will use the most clearly understandable language possible in stating their child's needs. This is consistent with the way many teams operate. However, there are also some who cling to technical terms often taken directly from evaluation reports. One such team insisted on the following paragraph from a psychological evaluation for their description of the child's needs:

His developmental pattern is a conundrum. He has problems in auditory memory, auditory closure, language encoding, language decoding, language semantics and syntactics, auditory/visual integration and more . . .

The IEP team must maintain a focus on planning the services the child needs. The more behavioral and direct the language used to describe a child's performance, the easier it is to determine what services are needed and at what level to begin instruction.

Suppose an evaluator has noted that a child has a "social skills deficit." That could mean any number of different things, e.g., a failure to appreciate jokes, chronic bullying, lack of eye contact or inability to carry on a reciprocal conversation. The more specific and generally understood the language the team uses, the better it can do its job of determining services. Sometimes parents feel intimidated by professional jargon or feel that they, too, should use it. A better view is that the entire team should use the most direct, ordinary language possible.

It may also be helpful for parents to think ahead of time about possible ways to address the child's needs. However, there is a pitfall parents should avoid. It is easy to slip from thinking about what a child needs to learn to do and any necessary conditions for that learning to thinking, erroneously, that the child, therefore, needs a *certain amount of a certain service*. One of the most common conflicts during IEP meetings arises when a parent says something like "My child must have occupational therapy (OT) a half hour every day." The other team members may believe that less than that, or another service altogether, would be appropriate. Far better for a parent to say: "Abby has had OT twice a week for several months and her handwriting hasn't yet improved. What can we change so that she will benefit more quickly?"

Parents may naturally wonder about what documents and other materials they should bring to the IEP meeting. Again, as always, the beginning point is to think about the child's needs (both for improved performance and for certain conditions for learning). If any of those needs are likely to be questioned by other members of the team, then parents should consider taking whatever supportive evidence they feel they need to the meeting, such as a private evaluation, a note from a previous teacher, or data parents have collected at home. Parents should present only as much written material as is essential to make the point, and highlight the key words or sentences.

If parents have a concern about the type or amount of service needed, they should bring pertinent recommendations or other supporting information to the meeting. The general rule is that it is better to have material at the meeting and not need it than to need it and not have it. The next rule parents should follow is to use whatever they have efficiently (i.e. have all materials well organized, have several copies of any materials to be shared, and highlight or otherwise direct attention to the relevant parts). No matter how much supporting material parents have, they should use only what is truly necessary. Anything else can be added to the child's file or shared with individuals as the need or occasion arises.

If parents and school personnel have followed the suggestions in this chapter, they will be ready to move to the next stage: A successful IEP meeting which results in a plan for providing an effective, individually designed free, appropriate public education for the child. Chapter 2 addresses how the team should proceed to develop an educationally effective and legally correct IEP.

Chapter 1

During the Meeting: Developing a Legal IEP

The Initial Considerations

When well prepared and well intentioned IEP team members come together, the process of developing the IEP can go smoothly, productively and even pleasantly. In this section we examine the process itself and all the steps necessary to complete a legally correct and educationally useful IEP.

As indicated in the first chapter, school personnel have the major responsibility for insuring the preliminary concerns are well handled—arranging the physical setting, making introductions and setting ground rules. Clearly, all team members, including the parents, should be on time for the meeting and in the best spirits possible ("we're all in our places with bright shiny faces").

IDEA '04 requires the team to consider certain factors: (a) the strengths of the child; (b) the concerns of the parents for enhancing the education of their child; (c) the results of the initial evaluation or most recent evaluation of the child; and (d) the academic, developmental, and functional needs of the child (20 U.S.C. §1414 (d)(3)(A)).

Considering the Child's Strengths

Commonly and appropriately, the actual IEP development part of the meeting begins with a brief discussion of the strengths of the child and the concerns of the parents. If the parents know before the meeting that these will be discussed, they can have a list of a handful of special strengths or "positives" about the child that might not be obvious at school but could be helpful to the teachers. Parents should resist the temptation to type up a 4-page single-spaced, detailed ode to the child's many capabilities. The impulse is totally understandable, but the true focus of the IEP must be on the child's needs. If the parent fears that some school personnel may be seriously underestimating some of the child's performance levels, that can be dealt with outside the IEP meeting, for example, in a parent-teacher conference or a private letter. Often there is barely time to cover the essentials in an IEP meeting, so it is important to use the available time on task. The kind of positive information about a child that can be helpful could include "She loves to care for animals" (perhaps feeding the classroom gerbil could be a great motivator for finishing arithmetic problems), "He is very appropriate with younger children and likes to help them," "She can glance at something and draw it almost perfectly," or "He has just learned to tell time and is so proud he can do it."

School personnel may also be able to note strengths or positive aspects of the child's performance unknown to the parents. Just as the parents should focus on strengths pertinent to school, so the school personnel may concentrate on strengths that are clear in school, but may not be as apparent to the parents.

Considering Parent Concerns

Parents must also be provided an opportunity to raise their concerns about their child's education. Some parents may be uncomfortable about social rejection of their child by peers. Others wonder about the expectations that are and ought to be held for the child. Some special education euphemisms may lead to such confusion. For example, the term "developmental delay" naturally leads one to ask, "When will she begin catching up instead of falling further behind?" When parents bring up these genuine issues, it is crucial that the team truly listen and respond with respect. Sometimes an expressed parent concern makes it apparent to the school personnel that parent counseling or parenting skills training is needed. Too often school personnel forget some of the specific, enumerated related services that must be offered when needed to assist the child to benefit from her education program. One of these mandated services is training for parents if it is needed. It may also be that parents need honest and candid counseling to understand the implications of their child's disability.

A possible abuse to be avoided in this initial discussion is making parents feel that the team grudgingly provided a required minute or two for their "concerns," followed by a checkmark on a form, and were relieved to move on quickly to other matters. To speak from the heart and not be truly heard is painful for anyone. It may be especially difficult for parents to talk about serious concerns if a large number of school personnel, some completely unknown to the parents, are present. This is one of many reasons the number of IEP meeting participants should be carefully limited except under extraordinary circumstances.

As parents express their legitimate concerns for improving the child's educational experience, they need to recognize that no one, not even the best qualified educators in all the world, can create time. If parents ask for extra time for all assignments and on all tests, plus daily tutoring in reading and daily speech therapy, the team has to prioritize how the school day is to be allocated unless the child is eligible for an extended school day, week or year. Even then, the team must ask about priorities. Does the team want this child to be practicing multiplication tables while other children are going to the swimming pool? The answer may be yes or no, but the question needs to be considered. There really is no such thing as "extra time"— there is time taken from one activity to use for another.

In sum, the child's strengths and the parents' concerns must be given serious consideration. At the same time, they are not the major focus of the IEP meeting. If it is evident that some parent concerns require further attention, it may be appropriate to deal with them privately or with a small group outside of the IEP meeting. The IEP meeting's central focus must remain on (a) the child's unique educational needs, (b) the services to be provided to address those needs, and (c) the expected outcomes (goals) of the services.

Considering Assessment Data

Many IEP meetings include lengthy presentations, sometimes read aloud verbatim, of several evaluation reports, including standard scores, percentiles, sub-scale scores and composite scores. A more helpful and pertinent approach is for the IEP team member who can "interpret the instructional implications of the evaluation results" to do so. Every IEP team must include a member with this expertise (20 U.S.C. §1414 (d)(1)(b)(v)). This allows the team to focus on what the assessments reveal about how and what the child needs to be taught. That is a primary concern of the IEP team. Standard scores are not.

Current assessment data may also be pertinent to the team's discussion of how much progress the child has made. Above all, the presentation of any assessment-related information should always be understandable and meaningful to all the team members, especially the parents. Parents can be given copies of the reports before the meeting and given an opportunity, outside of the meeting, to ask for any clarification they might desire. It is important that parents have the chance to do this, but it need not be at an IEP meeting. What is relevant to the team is the information about the *instructional implications* of assessment data.

Parents may have independent evaluations to share with the rest of the team. These must be considered. Parents often report feeling their evaluations were not given the serious attention they deserve. The level of expertise in these reports is often very high and should not be given short shrift.

> *"... [B]ecause the school district failed to consider the recommendations of persons who were the most knowledgeable about the child, it failed its 'duty' to conduct a meaningful meeting ... and it [therefore] did not develop a complete and sufficiently individualized educational program ..." (W.G. v. Bd. of Trustees, 960 F. 2d 1470 (9th Cir. 1992))*

Considering the Child's Needs

The most important part of every IEP meeting, beyond any doubt, is the team coming to agreement about the child's academic, developmental, and functional needs. The child's needs have always been the central focus of every IEP; however, it was not until the 2004 amendments to IDEA that Congress explicitly required the evaluation/eligibility team to determine "the educational needs of the child" (20 U.S.C. §1414 (b)(4)(A)), and the IEP team to consider "the academic, developmental, and functional needs of the child" (20 U.S.C. §1414 (d)(3)(A)). IEP teams should insist on having access to the needs determination that was to have been done by the evaluation/eligibility team. This can be a helpful starting place for the IEP team and may even be a complete and satisfactory listing of all the child's needs. All children who need special education have some kind of performance deficit; for example, they need to have a better level of performance in reading comprehension, social skills, upper body strength, or expressive language or to be more organized, or more patient. Many children who need special education also need certain conditions for learning, such as a quiet area, repetition of instructions or musical accompaniment to rote learning. Although we often say, in a manner of speaking, "She needs speech therapy" or "He needs a 1:1 aide" or "He needs physical therapy daily," it is very helpful at this "needs consideration" stage of IEP development to avoid these intervention needs and think only about the performance and learning condition needs. This is because services will be considered later and because saying, "He needs X service" tends to limit our thinking about how to address the need to that one service. There may be other, better ways to intervene than with X service.

Considering Special Factors

In addition to the child's strengths, the parents' educational concerns, assessments, and the child's needs, IDEA '04 mandates that the IEP team also consider (a) behaviors that impede the learning of the child or others, (b) limited English proficiency, (c) a visual impairment, (d) communication needs, and (e) assistive technology needs (20 U.S.C. §1414 (d)(3)(B)).

Behavior intervention plans

If a child's behavior interferes with his or her own learning or that of other children, or if the IEP team has reason to believe that discipline may become an issue, then the team should develop a behavior intervention plan (BIP).[8] IDEA '04 is silent about the form and content of a BIP except for the one requirement that it must include "positive" interventions. The statute states that "in case of a child whose behavior impedes the child's learning or that of others, consider the use of positive behavioral interventions and supports, and other strategies, to address that behavior" (20 U.S.C. §1414 (d)(3)(B)(i)).

In times not too far past, and still present in some LEAs, the prevailing understanding of a behavior plan was simply a brief listing of negative consequences to be applied if the child misbehaved. Commonly, the list culminated in the child being removed from school. BIPs often called for a parent to come to school to pick up the child. Some school personnel wrongly believed that this kind of coerced removal by the parent didn't count against the limited suspension time available to the LEA before additional IDEA protections had to be granted to the child in discipline matters.

Since IDEA '04 does not provide detailed guidelines or requirements for a BIP, we must look to the overall intent of IDEA '04 that the services provided to eligible children be effective, that is, that BIPs result in desirable behavior change. Developing an effective BIP with positive interventions requires specific training and experience that might mean including an additional person at the IEP meeting. An important way for parents to contribute to obtaining a good BIP for their child is to ask who at the meeting is skilled in developing BIPs. If it is necessary to have a brief

---

[8]The statute says that a behavior intervention plan (BIP), including positive interventions, must be considered (not "written"). However, IDEA '04 also requires a functional behavior assessment if the child gets into a serious disciplinary situation and a BIP was not previously developed (20 U.S.C. §1414 (d)(3)(B)(i)). For this reason and because it is good special education practice, the authors strongly recommend that a written BIP be developed as part of the IEP whenever the team believes behavior is or might become a problem.

delay or to reconvene later to have a BIP expert available (perhaps by speaker phone, fax, or e-mail, if not in person), that should be done.

At a minimum, an effective BIP will include (a) the behavior to be changed, (b) the desired replacement behavior, (c) the positive consequences to follow the desired behavior, and (d) how the desired behavior will be taught (e.g., by modeling). Bateman and Golly (2003) have provided detailed information on creating effective BIPs. Their book includes many actual examples of simple, direct, and effective BIPs. A brief summary of the steps involved in developing effective BIPs has also been included in this book in Appendix A for the reader's convenience.

Limited English proficiency

IDEA '04 requires that if a child has limited proficiency in English, then his or her language needs, as they relate to the IEP, must be considered (20 U.S.C. §1414 (d)(3)(B)(ii)). This requirement clearly applies to children for whom English is a second language and who are still developing fluency in English. It appears to also apply to children with serious language disorders that result in limited language proficiency, even if English is the first and only language. For such a child, this consideration could lead to instruction in a picture-based communication system, perhaps to signing, or to other accommodations or interventions.

Recently, the family of an eight-year old girl who has limited English proficiency (receptive and expressive language test scores ranged from a two- to a four-year old level) requested assistance to determine her proper placement in school. The girl had been adopted at age five and a half. From her birth until her adoption she had been in an orphanage in a culture where girls are never assertive and seldom speak at all, except in response to adults. This eight-year old spoke only three or four words.

This little girl presents a difficult, but not uncommon diagnostic picture. In considering the limited English proficiency of such a child, the IEP team must look at several factors—limited exposure to her first language, cultural expectations, only two and a half years of English-learning opportunity coming after age 5, and the real possibility of a language disorder which has affected her learning in both languages.

In recent years, increased attention is being given to the complexities of teaching English to children from a variety of backgrounds and situations. However, the intersection of language learning and special education remains difficult for many

IEP teams, as well as teachers and evaluators. Necessary expertise should be sought when the team needs assistance.

Braille

IDEA '04 requires that Braille instruction and use shall be provided to children with visual impairments unless the IEP team determines that Braille is not appropriate:

> **In the case of a child who is blind or visually impaired**, *provide for instruction in Braille and the use of Braille unless the IEP team determines, after an evaluation of the child's reading and writing skills, needs, and appropriate reading and writing media (including an evaluation of the child's future needs for instruction in Braille or the use of Braille), that instruction in Braille or the use of Braille is not appropriate for the child. (20 U.S.C. §1414 (d)(3)(B)(iii))*

The unusual specificity of this requirement may be puzzling without a bit of history. More than a half century ago a condition called retrolental fibroplasia (RF), caused by excessive concentrations of oxygen in incubators[9], resulted in permanent and usually total blindness in tens of thousands of premature infants throughout the United States. Special education responded by training thousands of educators for these children with visual impairments, preparing the educators to teach Braille and to provide educational materials in Braille. However, as years went by, the cause of RF was discovered, the oxygen levels were properly monitored, and soon retrolental fibroplasia became rare. The specialized programs and teachers that were so essential in the 1950s and 60s all but disappeared. This decline in Braille availability was probably fostered by inclusive practices and by the belief that technology would replace Braille, as well as by the decreased numbers of blind children.[10]

The decline in Braille availability and instruction became so severe and so detrimental to the education of blind children that the federal response was to create, in IDEA '04, a presumption[11] that a severely visually impaired child needs and should receive instruction in Braille. Any IEP team decision to the contrary must be based on an evaluation of that child's particular reading and writing skills and needs.

---

[9] The excessive oxygen damaged the developing vascular system that nourished the infant's retina, causing the retina to die and detach, thus "retrolental fibroplasia" (literally, behind the lens, a fibrous mass).

[10] The blind community, like the Deaf community, has made it clear through organizations and publications that it prefers this direct terminology to the politically correct "persons who have blindness or deafness," and we respect that position.

[11] In law, a "presumption" is a proposition treated as true, unless or until proven otherwise.

In addition to the importance of this requirement for the blind child's special education program and IEP development, it signals another important principle. Braille is a method of converting printed or spoken words (and more) into combinations of six raised dots arranged in a standard pattern. Similarly, discrete trial training (or ABA or Lovaas) is a method for teaching specific behaviors to children with autism, and Orton-Gillingham is a method for teaching the conversion of written English symbols into speech, that is, teaching reading. The statute creating a presumption in favor of Braille illustrates for every IEP team that there are children for whom a specific methodology not only can be considered by the IEP team, but sometimes must be. More will be said later about this controversial and important subject of methodology and the IEP.

Communication Needs

The requirement that the team consider the communication needs of each child has two distinct parts. First, the IEP team should consider the communication needs of every child, including, for example, the difficult case mentioned earlier of the child with limited English proficiency. The second part of the statute requires an individualized examination of the particular situation of each Deaf or hearing impaired child:

Consider the communication needs of the child, and in the case of a child who is deaf or hard of hearing, consider the child's language and communication needs, opportunities for direct communications with peers and professional personnel in the child's language and communication mode, academic level, and full range of needs, including opportunities for direct instruction in the child's language and communication mode. (20 U.S.C §1414 (d)(3)(B)(iv))

The requirement is broader than that dealing with limited English proficiency, as it encompasses all children and requires an examination of all needs related to communication. The specificity of the statutory wording regarding the communication needs of Deaf children and those with other hearing impairments also has a bit of history, as does the Braille requirement. In recent times, some school systems offered only one communication mode for Deaf children, such as cued speech, total communication or an oral method. All Deaf children were channeled into that one communication mode, without regard to parental preference, the language of the home, the child's needs or previous language experience. This single forced mode of communication was simply not acceptable to the Deaf community. The current requirement is the result of that dissatisfaction, and it makes clear that the IEP team must look at all the relevant factors and may not limit the language being used to the one method or mode the LEA has most readily available. As in all other aspects of IEP development, the child's needs are paramount and the LEA's job is to *make available* what is necessary to address those needs. This is, of course, a total reversal of the pre-IDEA era when schools could legally offer whatever, if anything, they had available.

Assistive Technology

The IEP team must also consider whether the child requires assistive technology and services (20 U.S.C. §1414 (d)(3)(B)(v)). For the team to fully appreciate this consideration, two IDEA definitions are crucial. The IDEA regulations define an assistive technology device as "… any item, piece of equipment, or product system, whether acquired commercially off the shelf, modified, or customized, that is used to increase, maintain, or improve the functional capabilities of a child with a disability" (34 C.F.R. §300.5). IDEA '04 now excludes from this definition of an assistive technology device a "medical device that is surgically implanted, or the replacement of such device" (20 U.S.C. §1401 (1)(B)). This excludes cochlear implants, as well as pacemakers.

An assistive technology *service* means "… any service that directly assists a child with a disability in the selection, acquisition, or use of an assistive technology device (20 U.S.C. §1401 (2)).

The Term Includes:

a) the evaluation of the needs of a child with a disability, including a functional evaluation of the child in the child's customary environment;

b) purchasing, leasing, or otherwise providing for the acquisition of assistive technology devices by children with disabilities;

c) selecting, designing, fitting, customizing, adapting, applying, maintaining, repairing, or replacing assistive technology devices;

d) coordinating and using other therapies, interventions, or services with assistive technology devices, such as those associated with existing education and rehabilitation plans and programs;

e) training or technical assistance for a child with a disability or, if appropriate, that child's family; and

f) training or technical assistance for professionals (including individuals providing education or rehabilitation services), employers, or other individuals who provide services to, employ, or are otherwise substantially involved in the major life functions of that child. (20 U.S.C. §1401(2)).

The primary focus of this assistive technology mandate is on the provision of assistive devices and services which will *improve* or maintain the child's *functional capabilities*. This is a broad mandate, indeed, and it invites the most reasoned, careful and cooperative consideration.

Many IEP teams do not routinely include a member with particular expertise in assistive technology. When it is evident that assistive technology needs to be considered, it is prudent (perhaps imperative) to have an expert at the meeting. If parents believe a particular technology device or service might be needed, it could be helpful for them to bring pertinent information to the team.

Between July 2002 and November 2004, only five cases involving assistive technology were reported in the Individuals with Disabilities Education Law Reporter (IDELR). This phenomenally small number perhaps suggests a low level of awareness of the IDEA requirements cited above, on the part of all team members.

Following the discussion of parental concerns, the child's strengths, assessments and needs, and the required consideration of factors such as behavior, communication, and assistive technology, the IEP team can begin to focus on the primary IEP concerns.

The Heart and Soul of the IEP Meeting

The heart and soul of the IEP meeting begins with the determination of (a) the child's unique educational needs (UENs), (b) the services the LEA will offer (special education and related services, modifications, accommodations, personnel support, and supplementary services) to address those needs, and (c) the progress the child will be expected to make with the provision of those services. The IDEA amendments of 2004 strongly and explicitly reinforce the necessity of addressing the child's needs, services and outcomes.

> *An appropriate educational program begins with an IEP which accurately reflects the results of evaluations to identify the student's needs, establish annual goals . . . related to those needs, and provides for the use of appropriate special education services." (Bd of Ed. of the Arlington Central School District, 42 IDELR 77 (NY SEA 2004))*

We call the present levels of performance in the child's areas of need the PLOPs. The services are what the LEA will provide to address the needs, and the goals are what we believe the child will accomplish if the services are effective. Thus, the sequence of the IEP development is from PLOPs to services to goals. These three elements are the educationally critical components of the IEP, and we should never lose focus on them. Sadly, many IEP forms are designed in a way that obscures the relationship among and the conceptual inseparability of these three components. Two examples of how a form can emphasize and highlight this essential relationship are shown in Figures 2.1 and 2.2.

Student _____

		Actual Performance Level and Date Assessed
Present Level of Performance:	1st Grading Period Progress Marker #1:	
Annual Goal : (Progress Marker #4):	2nd Grading Period Progress Marker #2:	Date:
Service: (Special education, Related Services, Supplementary Aids and Services, Assistive Technology, Modifications/ Accommodations, and Support for Personnel)	3rd Grading Period Progress Marker #3:	Date:
How Progress toward Annual Goal will be reported to parents:		Date:

Fig. 2.1 Sample Partial IEP Format

Unique Education Needs, Characteristics, and Present Levels of Performance	Special Education, Related Services, Supplemental Aids & Services, Assistive Technology, Program Modifications, Support for Personnel	Measurable Annual Goals & Progress Markers • to enable students to participate in the general curriculum • to meet other needs resulting from the disability
Danny is a fourth grader with L.D.		
1. Danny reads aloud very well, but he does not comprehend much of the stories. PLOP–Answers 0% of oral comprehension questions correctly during reading group (5-8 opportunities) and answers 50% of comprehension questions correctly in the workbook (10-15 opportunities)	1. Danny will be instructed from a highly structured, direct instructional reading program in a small group setting for 60 minutes daily.	1. Goal–By March 1st, Danny will answer 100% of oral comprehension questions correctly during reading group (5-8) and answer 95% of comprehension questions correctly in the workbook (10-15). P.M. 1–By November 30th, answer 25% of oral comprehension questions and 70% of comprehension questions correctly. P.M. 2–By December 30th, answer 50% of oral comprehension questions and 80% of comprehension questions correctly. P.M. 3–By January 30th, answer 75% of oral comprehension questions and 90% of comprehension questions correctly.
2. Danny spells very poorly. PLOP–Spells 3/20 words correctly on a probe with comparable words randomly selected from Spelling Mastery B.	2. Danny will be taught from Spelling Mastery B in a small group setting for 25 minutes, 5 times a week.	2. Goal–By June 10th, Danny will be able to spell 20/20 words correctly on a probe with comparable words randomly selected from Spelling Mastery B. P.M. 1–By January 10th, Danny will spell 7/20 words correctly. P.M. 2–By March 10th, Danny will spell 12/20 words correctly. P.M. 3–By May 10th, Danny will spell 17/20 words correctly.

Fig. 2.2 Example of a different partial IEP form completed

3. Danny acts silly, disrupts the small group often, and is sent from the group regularly for his actions. PLOP–Danny is sent out of the group for disruptive behavior at least once a day.	3. Danny will receive a silver star for not acting out in each small group, and a check mark if he does act out. If Danny does exceptionally well in the group, he will get a gold star. If he gets a check in the group, he will have to make lessons up during recess time and a notification will be sent home. If he gets all silver stars during the day, he will have the choice of a variety of rewards. For every gold star that Danny gets, he moves closer to getting a larger reward. All of the activities mentioned above will be carried out in the resource room; the rest of Danny's day will be spent in the regular fourth grade classroom.	3. Goal–By March 1st, Danny will receive silver stars for all of his groups throughout the day, and will receive at least five gold stars a week. P.M. 1–By January 1st, he will receive less than three checks a week. P.M. 2–By February 1st, he will receive no more than one check a week, and earn at least 3 stars a week.

Fig. 2.2 Example of partial IEP form completed. (Reprinted with permission from Sopris West.)

Regardless of how awkward an IEP form may make it for the team to address systematically and sequentially (a) the child's needs and present levels of performance, (b) the services to address each need, and (c) the expected progress, the wise team will find a way to do it. Only then does the IEP process have a logical progression and consistency.

UENs and PLOPs

When advised that the most critical step in IEP development is the determination of the child's unique educational needs (UENs)[12], some experienced IEP team members inevitably comment that "We can't operate that way because there isn't a place on our IEP form to put the child's UENs." It is true that many IEP forms hinder the process and obscure what is important. This is why it is so critical for all team members, especially the parents, to understand the essence of the IEP and to know how to produce a meaningful IEP in spite of the form. Regardless of the IEP form, IDEA mandates that the team must address the child's UENs. These UENs will be of two types—(a) the child *needs certain conditions* in order to learn and (b) the child *needs to learn to improve* certain performances, skills or tasks, for example, to become better at reading, anger management, making eye contact or sharing.

Needs Certain Conditions for Learning

Information about conditions necessary for learning comes typically from assessments, from teachers who know the child well and from parents. Expert clinical evaluations will often contain such observations as the child "needs a distraction-free environment," "needs 1:1 introduction to new material," "needs immediate corrective feedback," "needs tangible, frequent reinforcers when practicing difficult tasks," "needs small group instruction," "needs total consistency in behavior plan implementation," "needs close supervision during unstructured time with other children"[13] and so on.

Legally, it makes little difference where on the IEP form these necessary learning conditions are included. What is crucial is that they are there (somewhere) and that

---

[12]The word "educational" is extremely broad in this context, and according to extensive legal authority, it covers social, physical, emotional, self-help, vocational needs and more. In no way is it limited to academic needs, although these are included, of course.

[13]Needs such as these are critically important to hearing officers and judges, and if such needs appear in a child's evaluation reports but are not addressed in the IEP, those failures can be (and have been) the basis for a decision that the child did not receive a free appropriate public education.

they are implemented. On many forms they can easily be included as "modifications or accommodations." They could be attached to the IEP as an extra page or listed as supplementary services. Where they are does not matter; that they are somewhere matters a great deal.

Needs to Improve Performance Level(s)

The second type of need is the child's need for improved performance. These are the needs that will appear on the IEP as "present levels of performance" (PLOPs, to us). Imagine that the chairperson of the IEP meeting is standing by an easel, or a whiteboard or chalkboard, ready to list the child's UENs as the group offers them. These performance UENs, like the previous conditions necessary for learning, come primarily from assessments[14] and from teachers and parents who know the child. The team members who know the child can be asked to suggest what they see as the child's major UENs.

Lance's UENs:

To:
1. Control his temper.
2. Write more easily, rapidly.
3. Memorize his multiplication facts.
4. Stop picking on younger children.
5. Follow classroom rules about talking out and running.
6. Turn in all homework on time.

After the list of UENs has been generated, the team can prioritize the most important needs to initially include on the IEP. Usually no more than about five needs or so, often fewer, are appropriate. If an important goal is accomplished and more needs remain to be dealt with, the IEP can always be revised to reflect additional needs. Experience shows it is more effective to concentrate our efforts on a few priority UENs at a time than to spread limited time and resources too thin across too many areas all at once.

---

[14]Sadly, some LEA evaluators are now being required to use computer generated test reports which provide no clinical observations of any sort and contribute nothing to IEP development except bare scores which have little or no usefulness. Qualified independent evaluators, on the other hand, almost always provide insights helpful to properly addressing needs.

The next step will often be to refine the list of UENs a bit, perhaps eliminating needs that aren't special education matters (i.e., they don't require "specially designed instruction"), combining some UENs, or translating some into more behavioral language (e.g., "be respectful to adults" might become "comply within 5 seconds with reasonable adult requests without using any inappropriate language").

Lance's list of UENs included "to memorize his multiplication facts." One might ask whether this involves special education. Lance is ten years old, the multiplication facts are taught in the third grade in his school, and he has not yet learned them even though he had the same instruction as other children. For these reasons he needs some specially designed instruction. More of the same is unlikely to succeed. In other words, for some children, learning multiplication facts is part of the regular curriculum; for others, special education may be required.

For many IEP teams the most difficult part of IEP writing is developing the required *measurable* (and to be measured) sequence from PLOPs through progress markers or short-term objectives to the annual goal. IDEA '04 changed the previous requirement that all IEPs contain short-term objectives to requiring them only for IEPs of those children (approximately 20% of the special education population) who take "alternate assessments aligned with alternate achievement standards" (20 U.S.C §1414 (d)(1)(A)(i)(I)(cc)). Generally, these are the children with severe cognitive disabilities. However, all IEPs must contain:

*(II) **a statement of measurable annual goals**, including academic and functional goals, designed to—*

(aa) meet the child's needs that result from the child's disability to enable the child to be involved in and make progress in the general education curriculum; and

(bb) meet each of the child's other educational needs that result from the child's disability;

(III) a description of how the child's progress toward meeting the annual goals described in subclause (II) will be measured and when periodic reports on the progress the child is making toward meeting the annual goals (such as through the use of quarterly or other periodic reports, concurrent with the issuance of report cards) will be provided. (20 U.S.C §1414 (d)(1)(A)(i)(I, II)

We will call the legally required, measurable description of the child's progress toward meeting a goal a progress marker. In every way—form, function and development—a progress marker is what we have previously known as a short-term objective or benchmark. A progress marker is a measurable and to-be-measured intermediate point between the PLOP and the annual goal. In the very common quarterly (every nine weeks) grading system many schools use, there would be three progress markers corresponding to the first three nine-week grading periods. The fourth progress marker would be the annual goal. See Figure 2.3.

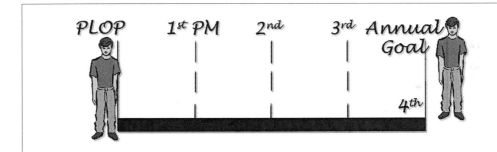

Fig. 2.3

We anticipate that in a few LEAs, the deletion of the short-term objectives for children assessed against grade-level standards will be welcome. However, some kinds of progress markers are clearly required and it is clear that the child's progress must be measured at least as often as that of nondisabled children. This is explicitly required by Section 504 of the Rehabilitation Act of 1973. We believe that common sense, efficiency, and good practice all lead us to treat progress markers as short-term objectives, and we strongly urge all IEP teams to seriously and positively consider this view. In the short term, doing away with objectives might seem desirable. In the long run, courts and hearing officers will find it totally unacceptable for us to use an ineffective program, method, or placement for an entire year without really monitoring (measuring) how the child is faring. To try to get by without measurable and measured progress markers is to court educational, legal, moral and perhaps financial disaster.

> *"The purpose of measurable goals and objectives is to enable a child's teacher(s), parents, and others involved in developing and implementing the child's IEP, to gauge, at intermediate times during the year, how well the child is progressing toward achievement of the annual goal. This information allows the IEP team to determine whether a child is making adequate progress, and, if not, to revise the IEP accordingly. Id. The United States Department of Education describes measurable annual goals and short term objectives as "critical to the strategic planning process used to develop and implement the IEP for each child with a disability." (Rio Rancho Pub. Schs., 40 IDELR 140 (NM SEA 2003))*

A finding that a child has not been given FAPE is the beginning of an LEA having to pay for private schooling or more. However, the most important consideration is that every child should be receiving effective services. Time is a precious commodity, never more so than for a child who needs successful intervention as soon as possible.

Whether or not we speak of progress markers, the IEP team must project a course from a PLOP to a Goal. PLOPs must be (a) objective, (b) precise, and (c) current. After all, they are the starting points from which progress is to be measured and improvement demonstrated.[15]

> *"... the diagnostic evaluation was eight months old, and thus could not be relied on to accurately reflect the student's present levels of performance." (Rio Rancho Pub. Schs., 40 IDELR 140 (NM SEA 2003))*

Starting points for measurement in other areas of our lives are such as 98.6° (a "normal" body temperature), 152 lbs. (weight on Jan. 1), milepost 33 on Highway 99 (where our journey begins), or a "12-minute mile" (today's running speed or lack thereof).

---

[15]At least since the 1997 IDEA amendments, the law has explicitly demanded demonstrated progress, that is, we must be able to show objectively the effectiveness of special education services. At least one major court recognized far earlier that the purpose of IDEA is "the achievement of effective results—demonstrable improvement in the educational and personal skills identified as special needs—as a consequence of implementing the proposed IEP" (Town of Burlington v. Dept of Educ. for Com. of Mass., 736 F.2d 773, 788 (1st Cir. 1984)).

The IEP team must convert needs typically expressed in non-measurable, non-measured terms into precise, objective and current descriptions of behavior. A PLOP must:

1. State the present level of performance. A rough guideline from limited case law is that the data should be no more than a few weeks old;

2. State the measured or carefully estimated level of performance. For example, Lance currently displays tantrum behaviors for 30 to 45 minutes at least four times a week;

3. State an actual, observable behavior, not a construct or abstraction; for example, not "has an auditory problem," but "doesn't respond appropriately to ordinary connected speech unless it is spoken very slowly."

Many common descriptions of educational status are not sufficiently objective, current, or precise enough to be useful as PLOPs. The following, for example, are not useful:

1. Kevin has poor social skills.

2. Ivan has a reading decoding problem.

3. Rashid's numerical skills are deficient.

4. Sarah needs to improve her listening skills.

5. Jessica has many negative behaviors.

In each case, to turn such a description into a useful PLOP we can ask (a) what does the child do that reveals the deficiency or problem, and (b) at what rate or frequency (i.e., how often) does the behavior occur?

We can turn each of the above inappropriate PLOPs into measurable statements by asking how we would know the child has a particular need. For example:

1. *How do we know* that Kevin lacks social skills? He seldom interacts with classmates and when he does, the interaction is usually brief and negative. In a typical day, Kevin has only one or two peer-initiated interactions which he ends immediately, mostly by name calling, and he initiates fewer than two peer contacts a week. Given this specific information, we can write a useful PLOP. For example, "Kevin has only one or two interactions with peers a week and these end when Kevin directs inappropriate language, such as name calling, to the peer."

2. *How do we know* that Ivan has a reading decoding problem? When we ask him to read grade level material, he makes numerous errors, stumbles over many words, including common ones, and makes wild guesses at multisyllabic words. He reads very slowly and only with much difficulty. How do we quantify this? By measuring his reading performance we learn his PLOP: Given third grade material, on five one-minute samples, Ivan reads an average of 25 words correct per minute.

3. *How do we know* that Rashid's numerical skills are deficient? Although he counts by rote from one to ten, when asked to count objects, he cannot correctly count more than two objects. This information is sufficient for a PLOP: Rashid can count by rote from one to ten and when given groups of one to ten objects each, he can correctly count two objects.

4. *How do we know* that Sarah's listening skills need improvement? When the teacher gives verbal instructions to a group, rather than to Sarah individually, Sarah usually doesn't follow the directions. How often does this happen? Sarah follows directions given to the group less than one time in five. That is the PLOP.

5. *How do we know* that Jessica has negative behaviors? She refuses to do what adults request, and if the request is repeated, she yells, throws herself to the floor and kicks viciously at anyone or anything near her. How often does this happen? Every time a direct request is made to her. The PLOP: Jessica refuses to comply with any direct adult requests made to her.

The baseline information provided ["short-term suspensions," "some sexual harassment incident," "people don't enjoy [his] company," "inappropriate behaviors interfere with his success in the classroom both socially and academically"] gives no measurable quantum of problematic behaviors, or measurable resulting amount of interference with K.H.'s social or academic progress; for example, how many times had K.H. been suspended as a result of the behaviors associated with the ED, how many friendships, if any, could be established as current for K.H., or how many instances and in what settings had K.H. been verbally aggressive. The information in the PLOP was insufficient to meet the requirement of 20 USC. §1414(d)(1)(A)(i) above. (Bend-Lapine Sch. Dist., 42 IDELR 25 (OR SEA 2004))

Too often, the PLOPs section of the IEP becomes a source of contention between parents and school personnel. This results from a lack of mutual understanding about what the PLOPs are supposed to be. Some parents bring many pages of typed, single-spaced information about their child to the IEP meeting. This information is often extremely detailed, highlighting everything their child can do. If school personnel feel that too glowing a picture has been painted, this can give rise to a concern that it will be hard to show real progress from what may be an artificially high level of starting performance. Parents naturally want the team to see their child in the best possible light. However, the PLOPs need to be much narrower, measured (or closely estimated by knowledgeable observers of the child) and *limited to those describing the child's performance in his or her areas of unique needs.*

Sometimes it is school personnel who propose the PLOPs section of the IEP, frequently in narrative form. To illustrate what has been said so far about developing useful PLOPs, let us look briefly at an actual LEA-prepared PLOPs statement. The IEP form this LEA uses has one full page (blank) for the PLOPs at the beginning of the IEP. Thus, this narrative is effectively isolated from the rest of the IEP. Consider how many precise, objective, current PLOPs are to be found in this extended excerpt from the PLOPs section of 10-year-old Donna's[16] IEP:

The following information is based on the Child Study Team evaluations and input from the parents and mental health worker. Donna has been on home/hospital placement. She has been receiving between six and eight hours/week of tutoring. She has been receiving one hour/week of mental health services.

I. Academic Achievement

Wechsler Individual Achievement Test (WIAT) results suggested that Donna's overall reading skills were in the high average range. WIAT results suggested that her writing and spelling skills were above the average range. An occupational therapy (OT) evaluation suggested that Donna's visual perceptual skills are in the low average to average range. She exhibited difficulty with fine motor, visual motor skills, and with alternating movements.

---

[16]Not her real name, but her IEP excerpt is verbatim and very real.

WIAT test results suggested that her math skills were in the average range. Voice, articulation, and fluency appear to be age appropriate. WIAT results suggested that Donna's oral expression and listening comprehension are within the average range.

[The WIAT and OT report are in Donna's file, so none of this information is helpful or necessary.]

II. Behavioral Data

Donna is a willful, spirited child who has a very low frustration tolerance. She has poor anger management skills to a point of violence at times toward mom especially. She is very compliant with her mental health worker and is communicating better. She has become more mature with adults. Her tolerance for academic tutoring has varied from no session to two and a half hours.

Tutor has to be very creative to maintain work effort.

Donna is a great kid who has a few behavioral quirks. She has a sense of humor, she is bright, and she can relate to others very well at times.

III. Learning Style

Donna's overall ability is within the average range (91) according to the Kauffman Assessment Battery for Children (K-ABC). Her simultaneous processing skills (100+7) [sic] were significantly stronger than her sequential processing skills (70=7) [sic]. This suggests that educational methods should focus on her ability to understand a task as a whole, use context to understand meaning, and to learn generalized rules by experience.

IV. Social/Family

Donna lives with her parents. She plays with other kids once or twice a week for short amounts of time. She has difficulty with large groups of kids. She enjoys swimming, playing with dolls, computers and reading.

V. Medical Data

Donna had four surgeries in [dates]. Mother reports that Donna began demonstrating emotional difficulties at age two following the surgeries. In [date], Donna was diagnosed with Anxiety Disorder NOS and ADHD, combined type. She has been seeing her physician for medical management since [date].

When such a narrative is used as the starting point for the IEP, the first job of the team is to find all the "needs" that are embedded or implicit in the narrative. One plausible needs list from Donna's narrative would be: (a) difficulty with fine motor, visual motor skills and alternating movements, (b) low frustration tolerance, (c) poor anger management, (d) variable work effort, and (e) difficulty with large groups of children. Notice that a relatively small proportion of the narrative relates to these needs. Of the five needs suggested in the narrative, none was measured in a way to provide a clear beginning point from which to assess progress. No harm is done (except wasted time and energy) by including the other information, but it isn't necessary since it is all available in much more detail in the assessments the team is required to consider and to maintain in Donna's file. The IEP should reference those assessments.

Some team members might question whether the visual-motor difficulty should be dealt with at all since Donna's reading, writing, spelling and math are all said to be average or above. Others might suspect this visual-motor weakness could play a part in her frustration, anger, and variable work effort. The judgment of the team must determine what will be done, if anything, about the visual-motor area. Compromise possibilities could include further evaluation of the area or reconsideration after a period of time.

The team might conclude that Donna's low frustration tolerance, poor anger management and variable work effort are all related. If so, the question is how do we know she has difficulty in these areas? Perhaps the tutor and parent quickly enumerate a variety of undesirable behaviors—yelling, stomping her foot, leaving the room, kicking her mom. The next question is how often these behaviors occur and consensus is quickly reached that they average about five times a week or once a day.

At this point in the discussion, someone might well ask whether a functional behavior assessment should be done to determine what function these inappropriate behaviors serve for Donna. The tutor observes that Donna refuses to continue working or otherwise behaves inappropriately whenever she is challenged by a task beyond her comfort level. Mom quickly adds that Donna's outbursts with her occur when Donna is asked to do something that is to her less desirable than what she is doing at the moment. The team agrees that she is avoiding what she doesn't like, and that gives them enough information to develop a behavior plan. If necessary, they will reconsider the necessity for an expert's functional analysis later.

The PLOP for Donna's inappropriate behaviors now can be written something like this: Given challenging academic work or a request to do something she considers less desirable than her current activity, Donna refuses to comply, displaying inappropriate verbal and non-verbal behaviors, about five times a week.

When the child's needs for certain conditions for learning and/or for improved performances (with PLOPs) have been established, the team is ready to consider how the LEA will address these needs. What special education and other special services will it provide? The measurable goals and progress markers the child will presumably be able to accomplish as a result of these services must also be determined. The sequence in which the goals/progress markers and the services are discussed is entirely up to the team's preference. It makes no difference to the "correctness" of the IEP. Our discussion will move from the child's needs to the services to address those needs and then to the goals/progress markers, but a team could choose to address the goals/progress markers before the services.

Special Education and Other Services

When the team begins to address the services the child needs, it is good to be reminded that the "I" in IEP stands for "Individualized." The IEP is an individualized special education document, and is not the child's total or general education plan. The IEP is to deal with the child's unique needs related to her or his disability and with the individualized special education and other special services to be provided, not with the regular education curriculum per se. However, the IEP must deal with the special education services that might be necessary to enable the child to access and participate in the regular curriculum. A child might need, for example, to be taught to follow directions, to work cooperatively in small groups, or to read at grade level so that she or he can participate in the regular curriculum. These matters should be addressed on the IEP, but the regular curriculum itself (often in the form of state or LEA standards) need not be on the IEP.

To be found IDEA-eligible, a child must require special education. That having necessarily been determined before the first IEP meeting, it then becomes the job of the IEP team to specify exactly the kind and amount of special education and the related services that are necessary to enable that child to benefit from the special education, and to spell out necessary supplementary aids and services, modifications and accommodations and personnel support.

The determination of what services and how much of each is to be provided is to be based solely on the child's needs, never on the availability of a service. If a service is needed, it must be made available. **No exceptions can be made to this principle**. The mandate to provide what is needed, rather than to offer just what is available, is central to IDEA. Any violation of this core legal requirement is extremely serious. That having been said, it is also true that under the law a child's entitlement is only to those services which are necessary to allow the child to receive some educational benefit, that is, to receive a free appropriate public education (FAPE) at no cost to the parents. The other side of the coin is that the child is entitled to all the services necessary to constitute FAPE. Again, no exceptions are allowed.

> *The determination of what services and how much of each is to be provided should be based solely on the child's needs, never on the availability of a service. If a service is needed, it must be made available.*

The difficulty, of course, is determining exactly what is meant by FAPE. "Free" means at no cost to the parents, "Public" means the education meets public standards, and "Education" is broadly construed to include interventions to address emotional, social, vocational, physical, academic and other needs (excluding medical services which can only be provided by a physician). The far more difficult term is "Appropriate." In 1982, when the primary purpose of IDEA was to provide access to education for children with disabilities, the U.S. Supreme Court held that appropriate means "personalized [individualized] instruction with sufficient support services to permit the child to benefit educationally from the instruction" (*Board of Ed. v. Rowley*, 458 U.S. 176 (1982)).

Since the 1997 and 2004 amendments to IDEA, most legal observers believe that this Rowley standard of 'some education benefit' has been raised; others are content to use the Rowley standard until the Supreme Court explicitly changes it.

A common misperception of IEP teams is the belief that a related service must be provided if it will "benefit" the child. The rule actually is that a related service is one which is "*required* to assist a child . . . to benefit from special education" (34 C.F.R.§300.24). Supplementary aids and services are those which "enable children with disabilities to be educated with non-disabled children to the maximum extent appropriate" (34 C.F.R. §300.28). Only the related and supplemental services which meet these definitions must be provided. This concept requiring the provision of *only* the necessary services is known as providing a "Chevrolet, not a Cadillac."

To illustrate, perhaps the parents have been told that some form of vision training would be good for their child. The question for the IEP team is not whether the child would benefit from vision training, but whether that training is *required* in order for the child to benefit from special education. Only if the answer is "Yes" is the LEA required to provide it. Therefore, the question becomes one of whether the child is benefiting sufficiently from special education without vision training. If so, the LEA need not pay for vision training.

Some school personnel seldom or never make recommendations about services they believe a child may need, believing 'superiors' have told them not to do this and fearing that to do so may obligate the LEA to provide the service.

Regardless of such policies or practices, the IEP team must consider the need for services as raised by parents or by outside evaluators. To consider is not necessarily to grant, but recommendations must be given genuine and serious consideration.

> *"While a school is not bound to accept all, or even any, of the findings and recommendations of an outside evaluator, there must be some alternate credible information to support its choice of a different educational model." (Chicopee Pub. Sch. 41 IDELR 87 (MA SEA 2004))*

If school personnel have pre-determined what will or won't be written into the IEP without genuine and meaningful parent participation, IDEA has been violated and FAPE has been denied.

Team members should brainstorm together to decide when, where, and how much service will be provided, and who will provide the services. IDEA provides clear directions about how the LEA should proceed if parents and school personnel cannot reach consensus about services to be provided by the LEA. This is discussed in detail later.

Brainstorming

A useful but under-used technique in reaching a genuine consensus about what services a child needs is for the team to brainstorm a variety of ways each of the child's unique educational needs could be addressed. For example, at the beginning of an IEP meeting, Chad's team recognized that he needs anger management skills, and they identified his present level of performance as three to five inappropriate verbal outbursts daily. Using a brainstorming approach, the team quickly listed several possible service approaches including group counseling, 1:1 therapy, social skills training group, a behavior management plan and a buddy program. The pros and cons of each for Chad were discussed and a better choice (one less expensive than the "standard" service) was made than if nothing had been considered except a list of the usual related services with the expectation that the team would choose one of those.

Suppose that Andrea needed improved reading skills. She is going into fifth grade and reads second grade material at 35 words correct per minute. Too many IEP teams would simply say "Let's put her in the resource room for reading 45 minutes a day." Sadly, this common approach reveals nothing about the actual service, if any, that will address Andrea's reading disability. A far more meaningful way for the team to decide what to do about the deficient reading is to brainstorm possibilities. After a couple minutes the team may have listed 1:1 tutoring, computer programs, Hooked on Phonics™ done by an instructional assistant, inclusion in a small group of mixed grade-level children in the resource room, and assignment to a third grade class using Reading Mastery™ for reading instruction. Now the team is in a position to seriously consider what services will fit Andrea's needs.

In sum, by this time in the meeting, an IEP team could have an agreed-upon listing of the child's high priority UENs and several possible ways to address each. Figure 2.4 depicts such a listing for Jordan, a distractible sixth grader:

PERFORMANCE NEEDS	POSSIBLE SERVICES
1. Needs better handwriting (PLOP: Jordan copies 18 letters legibly in one minute)	1. (a) occupational therapy, (b) drill with rewards for fluency and legibility, or (c) keyboard instruction
2. Consistency in completing homework (PLOP: Jordan submits 25-50% of his homework assignments.)	2. (a) reduce homework, (b) use notebook organizer, or (c) set up planned consequences for both completion and non-completion.
LEARNING CONDITIONS NEEDED	
1. Quiet, few auditory distractions	3. (a) carpet the classroom, (b) switch classrooms, (c) build a portable noise reduction cubicle, or (d) provide earplugs for Jordan

Fig. 2.4 Jordan's UENs (Performance and Conditions for Learning) and Possible Services

With such a brainstormed list, the process of selecting a service can be truly participatory and can result in agreement beyond that reached when only one possible service is considered.

When, where and how much service?

For each service and modification, the IEP team must also specify its beginning date, frequency, location and duration. Differences of opinion frequently arise over the amount of service to be provided. The amount of service must be individualized to meet the child's need and may not be the result of any other policy or practice, such as "We provide 30 minutes of group speech therapy weekly," or "Our extended school year offering is a regular six-week summer school." If a child needs daily 1:1 language therapy or schooling 52 weeks a year in order to receive FAPE, that is what must be provided. The fundamental impetus behind IDEA and FAPE is that public schools must provide what is needed, without regard to what is currently available. Prior to IDEA, schools were free, absent state law, to provide only what they had available. Too often that was nothing.

One important source of information to be used in determining the necessary amount of a service is the progress the child has been making with whatever past service was provided, if any. If progress was not sufficient, either more service or a different service must be considered. An equally or even more important source of guidance is provided by experts in the field. For example, one of the leading reading experts in the world is neuroscientist Dr. Sally Shaywitz. Shaywitz (2003) has reported that children with reading disabilities may require "as much as 150 to 300 hours of intensive instruction (at least ninety minutes a day for most school days over a one-to-three year period)" (p. 259) "delivered by a highly qualified teacher in a group of three or no larger than four students" (p. 258). Too few children served under IDEA in public school programs receive anything like this amount and quality of reading help. That is why generally "public school programs for children with reading disability are failures" (Shaywitz, 2003, p. 281).[17]

Who provides the service?

A question which frequently arises during an IEP meeting is who will provide a certain service. The general rule under IDEA has been that the LEA has the authority to assign any qualified (by state standards) person to provide a service. Parental input about particular providers should be welcome and taken into account, but the decision is ordinarily the LEA's. Under an exceptional circumstance, the parent might prevail, however. If, for example, a child had been in intensive therapy with one professional and was at a critical stage in therapy where continuity was vital, the parent might be able to show that that particular therapist was a necessary part of FAPE. A child struggling with gender identity might be allowed by a hearing officer to have a therapist of the appropriate sex. However, these extreme circumstances are unusual.

Most commonly a concern arises about the style, the methods, or the level of expertise of the service provider. Suppose that every evaluator of six-year-old Josh has written that he needs to be in a highly structured classroom. Josh's parents learn that first grade teacher Jones runs a very structured class while first grade teacher Smith practices a child-centered, permissive, discovery-learning approach. At the IEP meeting, Josh's parents request that he be placed in Jones' room, but the

[17]For more information on this exceptional resource, see references, page 133.

principal says she assigns all children to classes and Josh will be in Smith's room. At this point, Josh's parents might suggest a trial period of a couple of weeks and then a re-evaluation of the situation. If this issue were to go to hearing, it would be very difficult to predict the outcome, but good practice, individualization, and the spirit of IDEA would support Josh's parents' request. The parents' legal argument would be that Jones' structured procedures are essential for Josh to receive FAPE. The school's argument would be that IDEA procedures entitle Josh to be in a regular first grade class, but which class he is in would be up to the LEA.

Another difficult issue is the level of provider expertise needed for the service to be appropriate. In recent years research has confirmed that a teacher's skill and experience in teaching reading to children with learning disabilities makes a substantial difference in the outcome. Shaywitz (2003) urges that anyone who takes on the responsibility of teaching reading to children with reading disabilities must "be a knowledgeable reading teacher or a teacher who has had recent training and experience in scientifically based methods for teaching reading" (p. 259).

Whether a parent can successfully insist upon having a truly qualified teacher for a child is problematic. Perhaps IDEA '04 will strengthen the parents' position in this matter, as it now requires that all special education teachers be "highly qualified," in contrast to the former lower standard requiring only that teachers "meet state standards" (20 U.S.C. §1401 (10)(A)). This new requirement went into effect on December 3, 2004 when President Bush signed IDEA '04 into law, although most of IDEA '04 went into effect July 1, 2005.

IDEA '04 defines a highly qualified special education teacher according to the *No Child Left Behind Act* of 2001. Under IDEA '04 a special education teacher is highly qualified if:

> *(i) **the teacher has obtained full State certification as a special education teacher** (including certification obtained through alternative routes to certification) or passed the State special education teacher licensing examination, and holds a license to teach in the State as a special education teacher, except that when used with respect to any teacher teaching in a public charter school, the term means that the teacher meets the requirements set forth in the State's public charter school law;*
>
> *(ii) the teacher has not had special education certification or licensure requirements waived on an emergency, temporary, or provisional basis; and*
>
> *(iii) the teacher holds at least a bachelor's degree. (20 U.S.C. §1401 (10)(B))*

Parents of children attending Title One schools have the right under NCLB to obtain information from the school about the qualifications of the teachers and paraprofessionals who work with their child. Parents also have the right to access the research behind the reading program being used to teach their child. It is appropriate to request copies of the research, complete citations to it, and/or websites where it can be accessed. Wright, Wright and Heath (2003) provide sample request letters as well as highly readable and accurate information about parent rights under NCLB. We urge all parents to familiarize themselves with this information. Their website, www. wrightslaw.com, is a must for parents of children who have disabilities and for concerned professionals.

Parents often have uncertainties about the appropriate role(s) of paraprofessionals[18] in IEP implementation. Paraprofessionals may assist in a child's education program, but must do so under the direct, close and immediate supervision of a qualified professional, and they may not have the responsibility for planning instruction. Their role for a particular child should be clear to the IEP team members.

> *Wright, Wright and Heath (2003) provide sample request letters as well as highly readable and accurate information about parent rights under NCLB.*
>
> *Their website, www.wrightslaw. com, is a must for parents of children who have disabilities and for concerned professionals.*

By virtue of the provision of a 1:1 aide over the three years in question, direct provision of special education services were diminished. The services of an associate may not replace special education services identified in the IEP. The educational and behavioral plans require development, implementation and evaluation by a trained professional. Isolated with his aide or sitting in his "office" the majority of the day with his associate would certainly prevent the provision of special education services to advance Michael toward attaining his IEP goals. (Linn-Mar Community Sch. Dist. and Grant Wood Area Ed. Agency, 41 IDELR 24 (Iowa SEA 2004))

---

[18]Sometimes called assistants, aides, associates, or similar designations.

When consensus is not reached

If the IEP team cannot reach consensus about service provisions, Appendix A to the 1999 IDEA regulations spells out exactly what must happen:

The IEP team should work toward consensus, but the public agency has ultimate responsibility to ensure that the IEP includes the services that the child needs in order to receive FAPE. It is not appropriate to make IEP decisions based upon a majority "vote." If the team cannot reach consensus, the public agency must provide the parents with **prior written notice** *of the agency's proposals or refusals, or both regarding the child's educational program, and the parents have the right to seek the resolution of any disagreements by initiating an impartial due process hearing (34 C.F.R. Part 300 App. A, at question 9).*

To repeat—the essential point is that if the LEA declines to provide a service that parents want for their child, or the LEA insists on providing a service the parents do not want, the LEA must give the parents prior written notice explaining the basis for the LEA's refusal or proposal. This notice must include a description of the action at issue, why the LEA takes the position it does, other options that were considered, every procedure, test, or record the LEA used as a basis for its position, sources for parents to contact to help them understand this part of the law, and more. This written notice must be in language understandable to the general public (20 U.S.C. §1415 (C)(1)).

School personnel should insure that the obvious intent of this notice requirement—to provide meaningful information to help the parents fully understand the reasoning and data underlying the LEA's position—is fulfilled. Parents should similarly insure that they have received and understand all the information this requirement mandates that the LEA provide to them.

A verbatim example of how one large LEA evaded both the letter and spirit of this vital notice requirement is shown in Figure 2.5. This is the actual notice a child's parents received when the LEA wanted to (a) remove the child from his small, private, special education school (a placement earlier ordered at LEA expense by a hearing officer), (b) return the child to a regular classroom in a large public elementary school, and (c) deny him a previously agreed upon extended school year program.

1. Description of the proposed or refused action:

> Team proposes program to be 30 minutes monitoring.

> Team proposes placement to be in the general education setting.

> Team proposes removing ESY for summer school.

2. Explanation of why the action is proposed or refused:

> Action is proposed to meet the educational needs of the student.

3. Description of other options considered:

> 1. Option considered to stay with program designed on [date].

> 2. Option considered to decline special education services by parent.

4. Reasons these options were rejected:

> 1. Team decision to monitor for success in general education.

> 2. Parent reconsidered declining FAPE in favor of monitoring services.

5. Description of the evaluation procedures, tests, records, or reports used as a basis for the proposed/refused action:

> 1. Discussion, parent and teacher input.

Fig. 2.5 Actual "Prior Written Notice" by a non-compliant LEA

This so-called "notice" from the LEA to the parent explains nothing. The pertinent facts in the situation were that (a) the child was severely learning disabled (LD) and had little to no chance of succeeding except in a highly intensive and specialized setting such as the one ordered by a hearing officer, and (b) the LEA had budget problems and was, therefore, attempting to return *all* children from court-ordered private placements (for which the LEA was paying) to the LEA's own, less-than-appropriate public school classrooms, regardless of the child's individuals needs or situation.

This so-called notice is barely intelligible, let alone meaningful or helpful to the parents' understanding of *why* the LEA refused to continue the private LD school placement. The parents had to go to hearing a second time to maintain the private placement, and they won. The total cost to the taxpayers of the two hearings lost by the LEA would have paid for more than 16 years of tuition to the private LD school.

In sum, when parents and other IEP team members fail to reach consensus on a service or placement, the LEA must immediately put its position and rationale in writing, according to strict legal guidelines for prior written notice. Parents then have the right to initiate a due process hearing, a complaint or mediation to resolve the issue. If the parents request a hearing, the "stay-put" provision of IDEA requires the present placement/program be maintained until the issue is finally decided by a hearing officer or court.

Establishing Measurable Goals and Measuring Progress

When IDEA first became law in 1975, one of its major purposes was to create access to education for every child who has a disability. When IDEA was amended in 1997, that focus was shifted from accessing education to ensuring that children served under IDEA make measurable and adequate progress as a result of receiving an effective program of education.

Children's educational growth can be measured just as their physical growth can be. Suppose we want to know how much Sean grows (physically) from his eighth to his ninth birthday. First, we must measure his height and weight on his eighth birthday. Without knowing the starting point, it is impossible to know how much Sean grew. Similarly, we absolutely must have accurate, current, objective and measured present levels of performance (PLOP) data for the starting points from which educational growth will be measured and the amount of progress reported to parents.

These goals were found not measurable and not in compliance with IDEA:

"K.H. will exhibit appropriate work ethic and behavior in school and home settings independently 90% of the time."

"K.H. will apply decision, along [sic] and problem solving techniques in school and home settings 90% of the time." (Bend-Lapine Sch. Dist., 45 IDELR 25 (OR SEA 2004))

The IEP must contain "a description of how the child's progress toward meeting the annual goals . . . will be measured and when periodic reports on the progress the child is making toward meeting the annual goals . . . will be provided" (20 U.S.C. § 1414(d)(1)(A)(III)).

"[T]he program reports which were provided—simple checkmarks indicating progress rather than regression or achievement of Student's goals—did not meet the requirement that the report include an analysis of Student's progress toward IEP goals and an analysis of the extent to which Student's progress would enable him to reach his annual goals . . . It is difficult to imagine how a report meeting IDEA requirements could have been developed in the absence of a statement of current levels of performance and measurable goals and objectives.

This failure to provide progress reports constitutes a violation of the IDEA's progress report requirements." (Rio Rancho Pub. Schs., 40 IDELR 140 (NM SEA 2003))

Without adequate, measured PLOPs, this mandated progress assessment and reporting simply cannot and will not happen, thus denying parents their all important right to participate fully and meaningfully in decisions about their child's educational program.

"Mother's participation in the IEP process was seriously impaired by the absence of a clear explanation of Student's current levels of performance in reading; of clear goals and objectives defining what progress could reasonably be expected within the next semester; and by the absence of regular reports which documented the rate of Student's progress toward his reading goals." (Rio Rancho Pub. Schs., 40 IDELR 140 (NM SEA 2003))

PLOPs that are not measured are as useless as "overweight" would be as a starting point to see if Chubby had lost ten pounds after an exercise program. See Figure 2.6 for examples of non-measurable and measurable PLOPs.

Not Measured PLOPs: Tory	Measured PLOPs: Tory
has difficulty in reading	reads third grade material at 42 correct words per minute
doesn't turn in homework	submits less than 15% of homework assignments
doesn't get along with other children	has no positive peer interactions beyond a one word greeting/response
seldom speaks	initiates verbal contact with teacher and peers less than five times a week
doesn't follow directions	follows simple three-step directions (sit down, clap hands, touch nose) correctly less than half the time
has a very short attention span	stays attentive for less than a minute given age appropriate toys or TV programs

Fig. 2.6 Starting Points for Progress Measurement (PLOPs)

"The child's IEP for the 2003-2004 school year fails to adequately describe the child's present levels of performance. Global statements such as 'memory deficits impact upon academic learning' and 'improve decoding, improve fluency' do not ... provide a meaningful picture of the child's needs, nor suggest specific deficits that need to be addressed." (Bd. of Ed. of the Nyack Union Free Sch. Dist., 42 IDELR 78 (NY SEA 2004))

Measured PLOPs are not only essential for measuring and reporting progress. They are also indispensable for writing goals and progress markers. Even well-intentioned teams often lack adequate training and experience in writing goals that can and will be measured. Sad experience teaches that progress toward goals is frequently not actually measured, even when it is measurable! IDEA '04 requires that progress be measured and that it be measured against the goals.

Suppose a young person who has an eating disorder has lost an extreme amount of weight and is beginning therapy. You, as an observer, are interested in whether the therapy is effective, that is, whether the young person becomes increasingly able to deal normally with food and eating. One aspect of assessing progress could be to weigh the young person at the beginning of therapy (establish the measured PLOP), set a target weight (annual goal in the same measurable terms as the PLOP) and establish intermediate, short-term target weights (progress markers) for evaluating progress and, thereby, knowing if the program needs to be changed.

Establishing a goal and writing short-term intermediate progress markers are just the same. Both the goal and its short-term progress markers must be measurable. That is where some teams have difficulty. If every IEP team had a "measurable goal expert," an IEP goal development discussion could go something like this:

Teacher:

Jeff's writing is so slow, laborious and illegible that it really interferes with his efforts to express his ideas or even to answer questions.

Parent:

So, one goal could be for him to improve his writing.

Expert:

If his writing were to improve, what would he be doing differently?

Teacher:

He'd be writing more, faster, and more legibly.

Expert:

Did you have a chance to give the class the one-minute copying exercise we talked about?

Teacher:

Yes. Jeff had the lowest score in the class. He was able to copy only 10 words a minute and 4 were completely illegible. The other children had 20 or more legible words per minute.

Expert:

So, his PLOP is 6 legible words per minutes (wpm) and the annual goal for him could be 25 legible words per minute.

Parent:

Why 25 when the other children are only doing 20?

Expert:

Some are at 20 now, and by the end of the year will be even higher. The goal of 25 may even be a bit low, but if Jeff can do better, we can increase it later. We want him to be able to write at an ordinary rate so his writing rate doesn't hinder him in more important areas, such as expressing his ideas in written form.

Teacher:

His PLOP is 6 wpm and his annual goal is 25 wpm. Now what are his progress markers?

Expert:

We provide progress reports at this school every nine weeks, so let's follow that schedule for Jeff. So, we need, at a minimum, progress markers for the end of the 1st, 2nd, and 3rd nine-week grading periods. The annual goal is the 4th nine-week progress marker. Let's think of this as a ladder with the PLOP being the first rung and the annual goal the top rung.

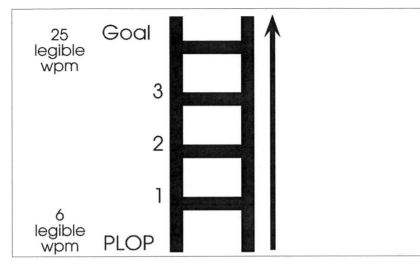

Fig. 2.7

The team has already decided to use a daily, timed practice plus reward for improvement as our intervention. We need to know promptly whether this intervention is effective for Jeff, so let's set a fairly substantial gain as our first progress marker. If the intervention isn't effective, we want to know that so we can change the intervention, the intensity, the provider or something else. Continuing an ineffective intervention is not okay. The other two progress markers we just set the best we can, using our experience, research and common sense. So, let's try this sequence: PLOP = 6 legible words per minute; Progress Marker 1 = 15 legible wpm; Progress Marker 2 = 20 legible wpm; Progress Marker 3 = 23 legible wpm; and Goal = 25 legible wpm.

Jeff also has some serious trouble getting along with peers. This is the next PLOP-goal sequence the team needs to establish. The discussion might go like this:

Teacher:

One of Jeff's biggest problems is that he just doesn't seem to be able to get along with his classmates at all. He has few interactions with other children in the class, and those he does have are almost always negative and inappropriate.

Expert:

Does he ever have appropriate interactions? I'm thinking that if he has very few that are appropriate, that may be why he has very few overall. The other children may avoid interacting with him to avoid unpleasantness.

Teacher:

I'd say that no more than one out of ten of Jeff's peer interactions is appropriate, if that many.

Parent:

That's consistent with what happens in the neighborhood. The other kids avoid playing with Jeff and when they do play, it quickly ends on a sour note.

Expert:

So, would it be fair to say that as of now, fewer than 10% of Jeff's peer interactions are appropriate?

Parent:

Yes.

Teacher:

I agree. That's about right.

Expert:

Good. So, now how often do we want him to have inappropriate interactions?

Parent:

Never! We hope he can learn appropriate ways of behaving, even in difficult situations.

Expert:

Good. We all agree that our goal is 100% appropriate interactions. Remember that when his dealings with peers become more positive and appropriate, they will also become more frequent.

Let's do a ladder:

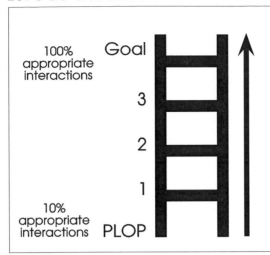

Fig. 2.8

As these illustrations show, it isn't difficult to write measurable PLOP—Progress Marker—Goal sequences. First, the team identifies an observable, measurable behavior that is acceptable as a reasonable indicator (almost never is it the only or the total indicator) of the behavior being considered. Next, the team gets the best information it can as to how often and over what period of time the behavior occurs.

To be useful, a PLOP—Progress Marker—Goal sequence must deal with observable, countable behaviors. One helpful question to ask is how would we know that Ellie's reading is better? That her social skills are improved? Her study habits are better? She is more respectful toward adults? Her expressive language is improving? What behaviors can we see (or hear), count and record that will allow us to assess progress? An observable, countable behavior that the team selects may not be the entire measure of the hoped for change or improvement. That is perfectly okay. The point is that it is an acceptable indicator, not necessarily the only one or the ultimate one.

The essential question the IEP team must ask is what behaviors can be seen that would show the child is or is not progressing or improving. One of the easiest and most productive ways for the team to approach this is to develop a measured present level of performance in the area of the child's unique educational need, and then to use the same unit of measurement for the goals and progress markers. The remaining step, too seldom taken, is to actually assess periodically how much progress has been made.

Reporting Progress

Measuring and reporting a child's progress is one of the most critical of all aspects of IDEA '04. The point of making a free appropriate public education (FAPE) available to every child served under IDEA '04 is that through FAPE the child can and will progress, that is, the child will receive an effective educational program. Parents, as much or more than any other team members, need to be sure that the progress reporting proposed on the IEP is objective, sufficiently precise and understandable.

. . . [T]he continued absence of a clear evaluation . . . of Student's progress toward measurable goals in the area of Student's greatest deficiency made it nearly impossible for the IEP team to devise a program which adequately addressed Student's needs. Both parents and other team members lacked information essential to devising an appropriate individualized plan . . . (Rio Rancho Pub. Schs., 40 IDELR 140 (NM SEA 2003))

Suppose the measurable annual goal for a youngster who has limited expressive language (the PLOP is that he speaks four words, intelligible only to his parents) is that he will have an intelligible expressive vocabulary of 100 words, all used when prompted and at least 30 used spontaneously.

If the proposed progress reporting system consisted of the teacher checking "emerging" (which seems to mean no progress yet, but we are hoping), "making progress" or "almost mastered," the parents and anyone else looking at the report would have almost no idea how much progress has been made. That is not acceptable.

Perhaps some would prefer a progress report by letter grade, with an asterisk to indicate a special education grade. Suppose the measurable goal for a ten-year-old was that she would always indicate her need to have a bowel movement by pointing to her pants and that her present performance is that she never so indicates and always soils herself. What information about her progress would be conveyed by a C+ at the end of the progress period?

The progress monitoring data presented by the school district is vague for certain IEP components and nonexistent for others. Few meaningful data are available to help an IEP team review progress or to confidentially [sic] convince this ALJ that the programs offered to Michael were calculated to provide meaningful benefit. In lieu of progress monitoring data for IEP goals the [Appellees] could have submitted teacher made tests, teacher observation, report cards, student handouts, and student portfolios as evidence of progress . . . , but no such evidence was offered. Instead, subjective judgments that Michael was "happy" or that he "loved his work experience program" were substituted for objective evidence of progress. (Linn-Mar Community Sch. Dist. and Grant Wood Area Ed. Agency, 41 IDELR 24 (Iowa SEA 2004))

Parents should be anything but apologetic in requesting measured, objective, and completely understandable PLOPs, Progress Markers and Goals. They are the key to knowing promptly and with certainty whether and how much a child is progressing and whether the special education and related services are appropriate. Progress measurement is absolutely essential to IDEA '04 working as it is designed, and without it the primary purpose of the law—providing effective education—is made farcical. The simpler and more direct the proposed measurement is, the more likely it is it will happen. Furthermore, if the PLOPs, Progress Markers and Goals are appropriate, the chances are very high that the parents themselves will be able to assess the child's progress should any questions arise. This has obvious advantages for all.

"The annual goals [in student's IEP] are measurable, provided one has the baseline data." (Hamilton-Sussex Sch. Dist., 41 IDELR 168 (WI SEA 2004))

Suppose a fifth grade child has difficulty in reading. His PLOP is 30 correct words per minute (cwpm) read orally in 2nd grade material. His goal is 100 cwpm in 4th grade material. His parents are vitally interested in monitoring his true progress and eager to support his remedial program in any way possible. It is easy enough to enlist a librarian's assistance in getting a couple of appropriate books at each of the grade levels 2, 3, and 4 ("give or take," as grade levels are approximations at best, but they work for these purposes). Every day after school, before a snack or before playing video games, the child and one of his parents can have one to five 1-minute each, timed samples of the child reading aloud from the appropriate book. The parent can count the words the child reads correctly.

Chapter 2

Our experience and conviction is that every PLOP—Progress Marker—Goal sequence should be so objective, countable, and precise that it can readily be envisioned and/or depicted as a ladder, yardstick, or similar model. If it is unduly difficult to draw such a model, something needs to be reworked.

- The PLOP tells us where the child is performing now in totally plain language;

- The Progress Markers tell us where the child will be performing when; and

- The Goal tells us where the child will be performing one year from now.

Parents should insure that they are completely satisfied with each and every proposed PLOP—Progress Marker—Goal. The team should avoid relying too heavily on subjective measures such as teacher judgment or observation. For example, suppose the team's first try at a goal for Jeremy is that he needs to "show respect for adults." How could one measure that objectively? The only way is to reformulate the Goal, PLOP and Progress Marker so they deal with countable behaviors such as "using inappropriate verbal or body language in addressing school personnel." Now the team can agree that Jeremy currently does this 5 to 10 times daily. The goal then becomes zero inappropriate verbal or body language toward school personnel.

An easy and key question team members need to ask is, "*How will we know* whether and how much progress the child is making toward this goal?" Only when this question is answered to the satisfaction of all have the essentials of both law and good practice been fulfilled.

Parents have a right and perhaps even a responsibility to recognize that genuine progress can be measured and to insist that the measurement/reporting scheme be as clear and understandable as weight loss, number of words read per minute, or number of widgets manufactured per week. Sometimes the jargon that professionals use in proposing goals and PLOPs can be intimidating. This goal was written on a recent IEP. The student will:

> *Comprehend and use written language more effectively* as determined by her use of written language during cognitive skills retraining activities as an Individual Educational Plan goal, as implemented by the Speech and Language Therapist, starting 1/11/2004, enabling progress and addressing her needs, in a small group setting, with visual and verbal assistance, using materials at her skill level, with 5% current achievement, with evaluation every quarter, with 80% target achievement completed by 9/15/2005.

In dealing with children's progress there is no need, ever, to accept such vague, unclear or overly technical language.

Other Important IEP Elements

While UENs, PLOPs, goals, and measuring progress are the heart of an educationally sound and legal IEP, there are other important elements that an IEP team must consider. Issues of methodology and multi-year IEPs as well as decisions about a child's participation in LEA and statewide assessments, accommodations and modifications in assessment, and transition planning when a child reaches the age of 16 are all elements that may need to be addressed at some, but not all, IEP meetings.

Methodology

Too many frustrating confrontations in IEP meetings have occurred around the issue of whether a specific methodology should be included in the IEP. Parents often believe passionately that a particular method should be used with their child, often because they believe that only that method has benefited him or her in the past.

School personnel typically believe that methodology need not be written into an IEP. That view was arguably correct until the 1999 IDEA Regulations were finalized and issued. An important change was made to the definition of "specially designed instruction" (which is the crucial element in the definition of special education). The word "methodology" was added to the definition of specially designed instruction. The U.S. Office of Education explained the significance of adding "methodology" to the IDEA Regulations:

In light of the legislative history and case law, it is clear that in developing an individualized education there are circumstances in which the particular teaching methodology that will be used is an integral part of what is "individualized" about a student's education and, in those circumstances will need to be discussed at the IEP meeting and incorporated into the student's IEP. For example, for a child with a learning disability who has not learned to read using traditional instructional methods, an appropriate education may require some other instructional strategy.

Other students' IEPs may not need to address the instructional method to be used because specificity about methodology is not necessary to enable those students to receive an appropriate education. There is nothing in the definition of "specially designed instruction" that would require instructional methodology to be addressed in the IEPs of students who do not need a particular instructional methodology in order to receive educational benefit. In all cases, whether methodology would be addressed in an IEP would be an IEP team decision. (U.S. Office of Education Analysis of Comments and Changes. Attachment to the IDEA Regulations, Mar. 12, 1999 (64 FR 12551))

In spite of this directive, many school personnel still decline to specify methodology on IEPs. A compromise that is often suggested is that parents' preferred methodology be described, rather than named. However, the difficulty with this is that it is very easy to claim that whatever is being done fits the given description. For example, when parents request a "multi-sensory" reading methodology, they usually mean the very specialized Orton-Gillingham method or one of its derivative programs. However, to many school personnel, any and every reading program, method or eclectic practice is "multi-sensory."

We highly recommend that parents invest energy in obtaining objective assessment of a child's progress with whatever methodology is used rather than just concentrating on getting particular services. If progress is shown objectively to be inadequate, it is then far easier to obtain the desired methodology. The combination of No Child Left Behind and IDEA '04 may eventually compel the use of only proven, effective programs for children with disabilities as well as for others.

Multi-year IEPs

IDEA '04 authorized approval of 15 state proposals for developing multi-year, not to exceed 3 years, IEPs. By law, no parent may be coerced into accepting a two or three year IEP. IDEA '04 requires the multi-year IEP be optional and parents must give fully informed consent before such an IEP is developed. Measurable annual goals and annual reviews are also required.

No one has yet had experience with three-year IEPs, so we can only speculate about the wisdom of this new provision. It would seem a multi-year special education plan would be least appropriate for young children whose condition is rapidly changing or for those whose needs are unclear. The advantages of a multi-year IEP over an annual IEP seem to accrue largely to LEAs and perhaps to parents for whom active involvement in the child's education is not feasible or desired. It is difficult to see how a multi-year IEP can be of more benefit to a child with a disability than a single year plan. Perhaps the time saving benefit to the LEA could somehow be translated into more time for direct teaching of children receiving special education. As of this writing, no state proposals for multi-year IEPs have been approved.

Participation in District/State-Wide Assessments

No Child Left Behind (2001) (NCLB) mandates that all school children's achievement be assessed, including that of children who have disabilities. Four types of child achievement assessment are possible under NCLB and IDEA '04:

1. Regular assessment using grade-level standards;

2. Regular assessment using grade-level standards, with allowable accommodations which do not invalidate the test scores;

3. Alternate assessment using grade-level standards; or

4. Alternate assessment using alternate standards. (20 U.S.C. §1412(a)(16)(A,B,C); 20 U.S.C. §6311)

The IEP team has the power and discretion to determine which assessment mode is appropriate for each child served under IDEA '04, except that NCLB, for all practical purposes, limits option 4 to only 2% of the total grade-level population in the LEA. Thus, the IEP team's discretion to choose this option may be subject to LEA or state guidelines and limitations, such as requiring that a child fall three standard deviations or more below the mean on intellectual ability to be eligible for option 4. Approximately 20% of children with disabilities will be eligible for assessment using alternate standards. The other 80% will not.[19]

---

[19]The NCLB Regulations do not actually limit the number of children who may be assessed against alternate standards. However, they do limit the number of such children who may be deemed 'proficient' in calculating Annual Yearly Progress to 2% of the total number of children assessed at the grade level. In all probability, most LEAs will try to keep the numbers of children offered alternate standards very close to the 2%.

Parents must be given clear and complete information about the requirements and consequences of each of the possible assessment decisions the team might make. Far too often, parents' lack of complete information leads them to seek what may ultimately be an inappropriate assessment for their child. Parents should know, for example, whether and how the type of assessment will affect their child's (a) graduation from high school, (b) type of diploma, (c) post-secondary school admission, (d) eligibility to receive certain accommodations or modifications in further education or employment or (e) eligibility for social programs or benefits.

Accommodations for Assessment Purposes

Some states have high school graduation standards which require passing state achievement tests with no or only specified accommodations being allowed. Some higher education institutions may allow a student only those accommodations in testing which were employed in high school and are documented on IEPs, unless the student's demonstrated needs have changed materially.

During an IEP meeting both the terms "accommodations" and "modifications" may be used in discussing program needs and for assessment. In the context of assessment they have special meanings (different from their use in instructional matters) and the difference between them is important. "Accommodations" would not (do not) improve the scores of nondisabled persons and are allowable, whereas "modifications" would (do) improve their scores and so are generally not allowable.

Allowable accommodations include a Braille or large type version of a test, using a scribe to record answers, giving extra time on a test where time is not an issue for nondisabled children, oral presentation of a test where reading ability is not being assessed, and similar accommodations that would not increase the scores of nondisabled children. Modifications which would invalidate the scores and thus not be allowable, would be changes such as having a test of reading read aloud to a child, allowing extra time on a rigorously timed test or reducing the number of alternatives on a multiple choice test. These modifications would improve the scores of nondisabled persons and that is why they are not allowed. They invalidate the test score, so there is no point in giving the test. Non-allowable modifications are also described as those that alter the test's content.

Transition Planning

For children 16 and older, the IEP team must include appropriate transition goals in the IEP. IDEA '04 states:

> *(VIII)* **beginning no later than the first IEP to be in effect when the child is 16,** *and updated annually thereafter—[the IEP shall include]:*
>
> *(aa) appropriate measurable postsecondary goals based upon age appropriate transition assessments related to training, education, employment, and, where appropriate, independent living skills;*
>
> *(bb) the transition services (including courses of study) needed to assist the child in reaching those goals . . . (20 U.S.C. §1414 (d)(1)(A)(VIII)(aa)(bb))*

The emphasis here is on helping children make successful transitions from high school to adult roles after high school, whether these transitions are to postsecondary education, vocational training, or employment. Congress recognized that helping children with disabilities make successful transitions to adult life often requires some years of training, work experience, and possibly instruction in independent living skills (e.g., budgeting and money management, accessing community transportation options, shopping, and personal and home maintenance) before the child is scheduled to leave high school. Transition services are defined as:

> *. . . a coordinated set of activities for a child with a disability that:*
>
> *(A) is designed to be within a result-oriented process, that is focused on improving the academic and functional achievement of the child with a disability to facilitate the child's movement from school to post-school activities, including post-secondary education, vocational education, integrated employment (including supported employment), continuing and adult education, adult services, independent living, or community participation;*
>
> *(B) is based on the individual child's needs taking into account the child's strengths, preferences, and interest; and*
>
> *(C) includes instruction, related services, community experiences, the development of employment and other post-school adult living objectives, and, when appropriate, acquisition of daily living skills and functional vocational evaluation. (20 U.S.C. §1401 (34)(A)(B)(C))*

The child's input (i.e., "preferences and interests") must be taken into account by the IEP team in determining transition activities. The child must be invited to any IEP meeting at which his or her transition goals will be discussed. If the child chooses not to attend the IEP meeting, school personnel must ensure that the child's preferences and interests are obtained through other means such as interviewing the child at school or having the child complete an interest survey.

Sometimes adult service providers are invited to the IEP meeting when transition services will be discussed. Adult service providers (e.g., Vocational Rehabilitation counselors, group home providers, supported employment agency personnel) are generally invited for the purpose of helping the team determine whether their agencies will provide any of the child's needed transition services.

Regardless of whether other agencies agree to provide transition services, the LEA remains responsible for ensuring that any transition services on the child's IEP are actually provided:

If a participating agency, other than the local educational agency, fails to provide transition services described in the IEP in accordance with paragraph (1)(A)(i)(VIII), the local educational agency shall reconvene the IEP Team to identify alternative strategies to meet the transition objectives for the child set out in the IEP. (20 U.S.C. §1414 (d)(6))

The transition component of the IEP is just that, a part of the child's regular IEP. It is not a parallel document, a separate thing, or a "transition IEP."

School personnel need to be aware that a child with a disability and his or her parents may not agree on postsecondary goals. For example, the child may want to live in an apartment alone or with a friend after high school while his or her parents may want the child to continue to live at home. Such differences may cause conflict during an IEP meeting, and the IEP team facilitator must be prepared to deal with the conflict.

Parents must also recognize that they and their child may disagree on postsecondary goals, but IDEA '04 is very clear that the child's preferences and interests must be taken into account. It is the child's future, and his or her voice is very important. It is the team's responsibility to put the support in place, through the IEP, to assist the child in accomplishing that future if it is at all possible.

Determining Placement

Usually the last decision discussed by IEP teams is that of the child's placement. For some teams, the placement decision is fraught with emotion and issues far beyond IDEA. Some people believe that every child who has a disability has an inherent human right to be placed in a classroom with children of the same chronological age who do not have disabilities. IDEA supports a somewhat different view and all team members should have the same understanding of its provisions. Under IDEA, every child with a disability is entitled to be educated in what for *that child* is the least restrictive environment (LRE). The LRE, in turn, is the placement decided on by the placement team (which always includes the parents but not necessarily all of the other IEP team members) according to IDEA requirements and its decision-making procedures. That placement may or may not be a regular education classroom.

A fundamental placement requirement is that children with disabilities be educated, to the maximum extent *appropriate*, with children who are nondisabled, that is, they are removed from regular classes only when *education there cannot be achieved satisfactorily*. IDEA mandates that:

Each Public Agency Shall Ensure—

(1) That to the maximum extent appropriate, children with disabilities, including children in public or private institutions or other care facilities, are educated with children who are nondisabled; and

(2) That special classes, separate schooling or other removal of children with disabilities from the regular educational environment occurs only if the nature or severity of the disability is such that education in regular classes with the use of supplementary aids and services cannot be achieved satisfactorily. (34 C.F.R. §300.550 (b)(1)(2))

Placement of children who have disabilities with those who do not have disabilities is a preference of IDEA, but this preference is limited by the requirement that the education offered must be appropriate.

Typically the placement decision is made at a meeting of the IEP team, even though IDEA actually distinguishes the placement team from the IEP team. The placement team must include (a) the parents and others who have knowledge of the child, as well as, (b) someone who understands evaluation data, and (c) someone familiar with placement options (34 C.F.R. §300.550 (a)(1)). Before placement is considered at an IEP meeting, it is important to be certain that the IEP team members who are present also meet these three placement team requirements. Usually this will not be a problem.

A second preliminary matter is the determination that the IEP itself has been completed before the placement discussion occurs. The placement must be based on the IEP (34 C.F.R. §300.552 (b)(1)). This requirement is especially crucial because the placement team's major task is to determine the LRE in which the IEP can be appropriately implemented. If the IEP isn't complete, the decision can't possibly be based on it. Many IEP forms include space for the placement decision to be recorded, but technically the placement process is, nevertheless, not part of the IEP.

A third preliminary placement matter is that all the team members, especially the parents, need to know that the required full continuum of placements is available:

(a) ***Each public agency shall ensure that a continuum of alternative placements is available to meet the needs of children with disabilities for special education*** *and related services.*

(b) The continuum required in paragraph (a) of this section must—

(1) include the alternative placements listed in the definition of special education under §300.36 (instruction in regular classes, special classes, special schools, home instruction, and instruction in hospitals, and institutions); and

(2) make provisions for supplementary services (such as resource room or itinerant instruction) to be provided in conjunction with regular class placement. (34 C.F.R. §300.551)

Too often, some team members perceive that the LEA may offer fewer placement options than the continuum requires or perhaps even offer no options. Parents sometimes report they felt only one placement was on the table for consideration— "take it or leave it." Under the continuum of placement provisions, each LEA is required to make all the placements on the continuum available as needed, but need not actually provide them all. An LEA may contract with other LEAs, belong to a regional service provider, or find other ways to insure the appropriate placement is actually available to every child. This requirement is consistent with the fact that under IDEA, no child with a disability has a legal entitlement to be placed in the neighborhood school. It is perfectly legal for an LEA to have, for example, only one program for children with profound cognitive disabilities and to have children from all over the LEA attend that program. On the other hand, if a child's IEP can be implemented in the neighborhood school and her education achieved there satisfactorily, that would be the placement. The IEP (the program) drives the placement.

The placement must be *determined* annually, while the IEP is *reviewed* annually. To determine the placement anew each year would seem to mean the team should start the placement discussion from the beginning, with a clean slate, each year.

One of the most neglected requirements in making placement decisions is that of considering any potential harmful effects of a placement on the child or on the *quality* of services (34 C.F.R. §300.552(d)).

In sum—the placement team needs to ask and answer a short series of questions:

1. Do we have the members necessary to constitute a placement team?

2. Has the IEP been completed?

3. Is the full continuum of placements available?

4. Can the IEP be implemented in the neighborhood school?

5. What, if any, are the potentially harmful effects on the child (of each placement considered) and on the quality of services that would be delivered?

The 5th Circuit Federal Court of Appeals has developed a widely used legal test or standard for knowing whether a placement decision complies with the LRE preference of IDEA. In *Brillion v. Klein* (2004) the court described that test, known as the *Daniel R.R.* test:

Daniel R. R.[20] adopted a two-part test, *asking 'whether education in the regular classroom, with the use of supplemental aids and services, can be achieved satisfactorily for a given child,' and if not, 'whether the school has mainstreamed the child to the maximum extent appropriate.' To decide the first question, we consider whether the district "has taken steps to accommodate the handicapped child in regular education." We consider whether the efforts to accommodate the disabled student are sufficient, bearing in mind that "the Act does not require regular education instructors to devote most of their time to one handicapped child or to modify the regular education program beyond recognition.*

Likewise, mainstreaming would be pointless if we forced instructors to modify the regular education curriculum to the extent that the handicapped child is not required to learn any of the skills normally taught in regular education.
The child would be receiving special education instruction in the regular education classroom; the only advantage to such an arrangement would be that the child is sitting next to a non-handicapped student . . .

. . . [In this case] the curriculum would have to be modified beyond recognition.

[The] teacher likewise testified . . . that in order to implement [his] proposed IEP goals and objectives, "the level would be so low that it would change the curriculum beyond recognition," and that she would be forced to operate "a classroom within a class." (Brillion v. Klein, 41 IDELR 121, 5th Cir. 2004)[21]

Other courts have slightly different ways of evaluating an LEA's compliance with LRE. In general, the factors examined include the academic and other benefits the child would receive in the placements under consideration and how disruptive the presence of the child with disabilities would be to the teacher and the other children in a particular setting. A child has no entitlement to a placement she or he disrupts, even with appropriate behavioral interventions.

---

[20]*Daniel R.R.* v. St. Bd. of Ed., 844 F2d 1036 (5th Cir. 1989)

[21]This decision has not been released for publication in official or permanent law reports.

In 1999, one further placement consideration was added to the IDEA regulations. Now a child may not be removed from an age-appropriate regular class *solely* because of needed curriculum modifications (34 C.F.R. §300.552(e)).
One might speculate, however, that major curriculum modifications would always involve additional factors such as excessive teacher time. Five years after that 1999 regulation, the 5th Circuit court observed that it is not necessary to offer a substantially different curriculum (from that of the other children) to a child with a disability in that regular classroom. In other words, the 5th Circuit court believes a child can be moved out of the regular classroom to where an appropriate curriculum is available, without violating the law.

Placement decisions are, and will remain, among the most difficult questions facing many teams. If the LRE were understood by everyone to be whatever placement is determined by the guidelines of IDEA, rather than always being a regular classroom, teams and children would benefit greatly.

In sum, two overriding principles of placement have always been that (a) the placement decision must be *individualized* to the child, as are all IDEA decisions, and (b) the placement must be selected from the full continuum of alternate placements.

Once an appropriate placement decision has been made, the formal IEP meeting is finished. There are other tasks which school personnel must conduct, including distributing copies of the completed IEP and monitoring the child's progress. These and other tasks will be described in Chapter 3.

Chapter 2

Chapter 3

Ensuring FAPE After the Meeting

Distributing Copies of the IEP

School personnel sometimes want time after the IEP meeting to put finishing touches on the IEP before mailing the parents' copy to them. IDEA requires that the school give the parents a copy at no expense to them (34 C.F.R. §300.345 (f)). If the IEP development has been difficult, the discussion heated or lengthy or for any other reason, the parents may wish to obtain a copy of the rough IEP before leaving the meeting and school personnel should comply with this request. If notes were taken during the meeting, especially if they are to be incorporated into the IEP, a copy of those should also be provided to the parents at their request. Of course, a copy of the finalized IEP must also be given to the parents.

An IEP is an "education record" as defined in and protected by the Family Educational Rights and Privacy Act (FERPA). FERPA (1995) generally allows school personnel to disclose education records only with parental consent. However, there are many exceptions to this parental consent disclosure requirement. One of these exceptions allows school personnel to share education records, including IEPs, with other school personnel determined by the LEA to have "legitimate education interests" in the record(s). Rarely does a dispute arise over sharing IEPs with interested parties because it is almost always in the child's interest that everyone involved with him or her have a copy of at least the pertinent portions of the IEP. If a parent has any concern that the IEP (or portions of it) are not reaching all who should see it, the parent can simply take responsibility for making copies and can personally hand them to the bus driver, substitute teachers, cafeteria monitors, playground supervisors, vice principal, security officers and more. Sadly, it is possible that some school personnel who have contact with children receiving special education may not be familiar with IEPs or may not know that certain provisions of an IEP (especially related to behavioral matters) apply to all school personnel, not just to teachers and related services staff. The crucial thing to remember is that parents are completely free to distribute and circulate their child's IEP or other education records as they please. FERPA places distribution and access restrictions only on educational institutions, not on parents or children.

Another reason parents should consider making multiple copies of the IEP is that if the child moves to another school, the IEP can be immediately available to the new school personnel, should parents so desire.

The critical matter for the LEA with regard to copies of a child's IEP is to be sure that copies are provided to (a) the parents, (b) the child's teacher and related service providers, and (c) in the event of behavioral provisions, to all school personnel who could be involved with the child. Further, school personnel should be sure the parents are fully informed of their rights regarding copies of the IEP and related documents such as evaluation reports which they might wish to share with others.

Ensuring that Services in the IEP are Provided

The first key to ensuring the provision of all the special services in the IEP is having clarity in the IEP itself. Suppose an IEP says the child will receive "270 minutes a week of special reading." Few of us think in terms of "minutes a week," so a first step is to convert this to hours, that is, 4.5 hours a week. That translates to less than an hour a day. Parents should confirm with the rest of the team whether that is in fact what is being offered and whether it is instead of, or in addition to 'regular reading.' If it is in addition to, is it the same program or a different program? If different, are the two programs compatible? The team should consider transition times and where they are in the calculations. If service times are given in minutes per quarter or semester, it is even more important to get a meaningful translation, usually to hours per day or week. How much is 120 minutes a quarter?

It is also critical to determine *where* a service is to be delivered, and sometimes *by whom*. Parents are sometimes surprised to find that an untrained aide is to actually provide a service, or that "consultation" services mean the qualified provider (e.g. the occupational or speech therapist) will merely speak with the child's classroom teacher and not actually provide any direct service to the child, or that "monitoring the child's articulation" is to be done everywhere by all school personnel at all times, with no one actually responsible for doing it or noting the results. The IEP team is responsible for ensuring that the IEP is clear about how often, where and by whom services will be delivered.

IEP teams should not include vague information such as "225 minutes a week of resource room" or "1650 minutes a week of special education" in the IEP. Parents should ask for clarification of such information and insist that enough correct, precise information be written on the IEP to allow one to know whether the IEP services are truly and faithfully being implemented. What is happening in the resource room? How many other children are in the room? What are the other children's performance levels? Does the resource teacher provide 1:1 or small group instruction? Does the resource room simply function as a study hall? Do the children just complete worksheets? What is the child missing in the regular class while in the resource room? How does the child feel about being in the resource room? (If the resource program is effective and the child is learning new skills, chances are the child will enjoy being there.)

Just as problematic is understanding what exactly is covered by the term "special education." To know a child is receiving 5 hours a day of special education is not sufficient. What is the daily schedule? How much direct teaching is done by the teacher, by an aide? How much diversity is there in the performance levels and needs of other children in each instructional group? What is different about "special education language arts" from "regular education language arts"? How much 1:1 instruction is included? How much small group instruction? How small is the group? Until all team members understand *exactly* what is being proposed in the "5 hours daily of special education," it is impossible for them to make a reasonable judgment about the probable appropriateness and effectiveness of the services for the child.

Monitoring Progress

Once a clear and absolutely unambiguous picture of the services that are being proposed is known by all the team members, the next step is to clarify exactly how, when and by whom the progress assessment will be done. It is not enough that the services be delivered. Under IDEA '04, those services are to be effective, and that is why objective, measurable and measured goals and progress markers are critical. It is never acceptable to suggest that "making progress" (or any version thereof) is a sufficiently objective assessment. It is not. If the IEP team has done its required job, the IEP will specify *objective progress marker measurements* to be taken preferably at least every nine weeks.

The statements of Student's annual goals and objectives in each IEP simply do not contain objective criteria which permit measurement of Student's progress, especially in light of the absence of a statement of Student's current level of performance. A goal of "increasing" reading comprehension skills or "improving decoding skills" is not a measurable goal without a clear statement of Student's present level of performance and a specific objective against which Student's progress can be measured. Even if present levels of performance were clearly stated, an open-ended statement that Student will "improve" does not meet the requirement (added by the 1997 amendments to the IDEA) for a "measurable" goal. The addition of a percentage of accuracy is not helpful where the IEP fails to define a starting point, an ending point, the curriculum in which Student will achieve 80 or 85% accuracy, or a procedure for pre-and post-testing of Student. (Rio Rancho Pub. Schs., 40 IDELR 140 (NM SEA 2003))

The results of the objective progress assessments should be recorded and evaluated against the original goals. For example, suppose one of Jenni's original PLOPs is: "Jenni has an average of five unexcused absences and tardies a week." The annual goal for this PLOP, "Jenni will average less than 1 unexcused absence or tardy a week." The team established the following three quarterly progress markers:

1. Jenni will average less than 4 absences and tardies a week by the end of the first quarter.

2. Jenni will average less than 3 absences and tardies a week by the end of the second quarter.

3. Jenni will average less than 2 absences and tardies a week by the end of the third quarter.

Here are Jenni's data from her school's office records for the first two quarters:

Table 3.1: Jenni's Average Number of Weekly Absences and Tardies.

Quarter 1	Absences	Tardies	Total
Week 1	3	2	5
2	2	2	4
3	4	1	5
4	2	5	7
5	2	2	4
6	1	3	4
7	1	4	5
8	1	2	3
9	1	3	4
Average			41/9 = 4.5
Quarter 2			
Week 1	1	3	4
2	0	2	2
3	0	3	3
4	0	1	1
5	0	2	2
6	1	2	3
7	0	2	2
8	0	1	1
9	0	3	3
Average			21/9 = 2.3

These data show that Jenni didn't quite reach the first progress marker but was nevertheless making significant progress. By the 2nd nine weeks she was well on track to reach the annual goal. The crucial point is that objective measurement, as required by IDEA '04, is the key to insuring that effective services are delivered. The emphasis in service provision needs to shift from "what service is provided, how often" to how *effective* is the service, whatever it may be.

As mentioned earlier, many parents invest heavily in obtaining a huge variety of evaluations and in securing certain amounts of particular services. In the authors' experience, the same energy directed toward obtaining regular, objective progress assessments goes further toward insuring the effectiveness of services. If such assessments show that the child is not making adequate progress, the intervention that has not been successful *must* be changed. If an LEA were to unreasonably continue a service that data had shown to be ineffective, that could be seen as not acting in good faith,[22] or having denied FAPE. Then the LEA could be liable for a private placement, compensatory education, or other remedies, perhaps even dollar damages.

Having opined that meaningful progress assessment is ultimately more important than the amount of service, it is also true that IDEA requires that all the services written on the IEP must be provided as written, or the IEP must be changed. When parents want to know whether the services are in fact being provided as written in the IEP, the most direct way is to ask. If there are admitted, significant lapses, parents should ask if there are plans to make up for the missed services.

One way for parents to monitor services more closely is to obtain the child's schedule for each day of the week and ask the child about the day. If, for example, speech therapy is scheduled for Wednesdays, from 9:30 to 10:00, many children will be able to accurately report when asked that day, whether speech therapy happened, where it was, and how many other children were there. If necessary, parents might enlist the help of another child, perhaps the child of a friend, who has the opportunity to know the comings and goings of the child of concern. It is important to remember that school schedules are subject to changes at short notice and because of unpreventable interruptions such as snow days. If parents and school personnel are reasonable and flexible, these issues can be worked out. Under ordinary circumstances, a service failure of a small percentage (e.g. 5%) of scheduled time will not be considered bad

---

[22]IDEA does not require that a child reach every goal, but it does require the LEA to act in good faith to assist the child to reach the goals. A failure to act in good faith could, in some circumstances, be or contribute to a denial of FAPE.

faith on the part of the LEA. LEAs, on the other hand, need to make every reasonable effort to make up lost service time, whatever the reason.

Another way parents can monitor their child's services and progress is to observe in the child's classroom. However, it is critical not to disrupt the program by excessive or inappropriate observations. LEAs vary tremendously in their openness to parent observations. If a written policy exists, it should be followed closely. Sometimes volunteering in the classroom is a good option. Whatever observation opportunities are available to parents of nondisabled children must also be offered equally to parents of children who have disabilities.

Parents should remember that knowing exactly *what is being provided* is not the same as monitoring the *effectiveness of the services*, that is, the amount of measured progress the child is making. Parents must receive progress reports concurrent with the issuance of report cards to all children. Progress reports must include progress toward the annual goal. Parents must not settle for less. Does a letter grade of B (with an asterisk indicating it is "modified") in reading convey the required information? An S for satisfactory? Making progress? Good effort?

> *... [C]ourts have been unwilling to accept school districts' assertions concerning the appropriateness of a student's educational program absent proof in the form of data ... (Linn-Mar Community Sch. Dist. and Grant Wood Area Ed. Agency, 41 IDELR 24 (Iowa SEA 2004))*

As was said before and can't be said too often, meaningful progress assessment is absolutely dependent on first having objective, measured PLOPs and then actually measuring the child's progress relative to measurable progress markers. Finally, did the child's progress, as measured, reach the measurable goal? If not, the service must be changed.

Reviewing and Revising the IEP

When a child is not making progress commensurate with reasonable expectations, it is essential to review the IEP and determine what is to be changed. Either parents or the LEA may request an IEP meeting for this purpose. However, the LEA is not necessarily required to grant an unreasonable meeting request. IDEA '04 now allows parents and school personnel to agree, after the required annual IEP meeting, that changes may be made later by developing a written document rather than convening another meeting (20 U.S.C. §1414 (d)(3)(D)).

Determining Progress Since Initiating Services

One of the most common scenarios leading to due process hearings and court is that of the failed IEP review. When there are no precise, objective progress measurements, school personnel frequently believe the child is "doing just fine," while the parents see grossly insufficient progress and ne'er the twain meet.

[I] n the absence of an indication of student's level of performance when the IEP was written, an objective 80% accuracy, measured by teacher observation, fails to meet the requirement that an IEP specify strategies for adequately evaluating progress . . . (Evans v. Bd. of Ed. of Rhinebeck Central School District, 930 F. Supp. 83 (S.D.N.Y. 1996))

Sometimes, in an effort to resolve the impasse, a whole new round of expensive and time consuming evaluations are sought. Few, if any, of the assessment tools typically used in these evaluations are capable of reliably showing small increments of change, and certainly not those changes made over a few weeks or even months.

Furthermore, many IEP teams lack the required member who has the expertise to properly interpret scores, to know, for example, whether a reading grade level score on one test can properly be compared to that on another. Or to know whether a child can continue to score lower and lower, for example, in percentile ranks, and yet be making adequate progress.

As has been emphasized earlier, being able to assess children's progress is central to compliance with IDEA and to providing effective special education. We must use (a) *measured present levels of performance,* (b) *measurable and measured progress markers* (short-term objectives) and (c) *measurable annual goals,* or we must admit that we are not serious about compliance with the law or about effective special education services. The purpose of both the law and special education itself is to insure improved functioning levels for children who have disabilities. Without adequate measurement, we cannot know or show that purpose has been accomplished, as figure 3. 1 (blithely) indicates.

The Hemispheric Measurement Challenge

RB:

Wait a minute here. All I really want is for Jason to be all he can be. That can't be measured.

LB:

What might you see within one year that would tell you he is on that path?

RB:

If he could learn to talk and to play with objects, rather than just with his own hands and feet and mouth, I'd know that was a step in the right direction.

LB:

Now we're on the right path. From here we can easily establish two measurable goals and two sets of progress markers . . .

RB2:

If Jessica could stop being a self-righteous, arrogant geek and act like an ordinary, 12-year old, maybe she wouldn't always be so isolated and unhappy. But you can't put that in measurable terms.

LB2:

Why do you call her a geek?

RB2:

She always has the right answer and blurts it out and she tells other kids they are stupid. Last night the family went out to dinner and Jessica jumped up and loudly told the people at the next table that they were crazy to say that states were blue or red, since states aren't any color.

LB2:

So, if we could decrease her inappropriate remarks to others, would that be a sign of progress?

RB2:

You bet . . . oh, I'm starting to see . . .

Figure 3.1: Two brief inner dialogues between 'Right Brain' and 'Left Brain.'

Objective progress measurement should always be appropriately dealt with in the original IEP and, if it isn't, the IEP review will be subjective, messy, and perhaps contentious. But all need not be lost. The review provides another opportunity to develop measurable (and to-be-measured) PLOPs, progress markers and goals. It may be too late to avoid all legal repercussions, but it can provide excellent damage control and get the entire IEP process back on the right track for the future.

How Much Progress is Enough?

The first focus of an IEP review must be on how much true progress the child is actually making. Assuming that has been established satisfactorily, the question becomes how much progress is enough? Parent and school personnel expectations are sometimes appreciably different. Any effort spent in coming to a common understanding of reasonable expectations for growth is well spent. Independent expert opinions can be most helpful, as can the view of qualified evaluators who have seen the child over a period of time. Too often we fail to specifically request this prognosis from all professionals who have relevant experience and training and know the child. We need their best opinions as to the rate and type of progress that may reasonably be expected. These matters are not governed by mathematical formulas, of course. We always need to allow for unusual, special factors and circumstances. Errors, if made, must be on the side of optimism. The exciting possibilities of growth beyond expectations must never be doubted. On the other hand, less progress than is reasonably expected, given the disability and effective interventions, should never be accepted.

Yet one more element in this balancing act is that children's growth, development and progress do not occur in a straight line. Spurts and plateaus happen. It is important, however, not to allow a plateau to be unduly prolonged by our failure to change or intensify the intervention.

Sometimes, school personnel fail to share with parents the kinds of information that truly speak to progress. Teachers, aides and others close to the child often have information far more meaningful to parents than percentiles and standard scores. For example, a school secretary, before an IEP review, spoke to Aaron's parents about how Aaron was now so polite and appropriate when he came into the office before or after school. At the beginning of the year he had pushed other children away from the counter and yelled what he wanted. Now he waited his turn and spoke politely, calling the secretary by name and later thanking her for helping him. The parents were delighted.

When we are attempting to evaluate the amount of progress a child has made, it is absolutely essential that we look beyond (and away from) primary reliance on standardized test scores with their standard scores and other statistical accessories. Let us focus on *what children do and how often they do it*. That will allow reasonable people to come to rational agreements or disagreements about whether progress is adequate for that child, during this time period, given these circumstances.

One of the few definitive legal principles in establishing the sufficiency of progress is that the determination must be individualized and take into account the child's own ability level. However, having said that, it is also clear that beyond that principle not all courts completely agree. Different jurisdictions have somewhat different standards for determining how much progress ('educational benefit' is the term courts usually use) constitutes an "appropriate" education, that is, how much progress a child is entitled to under IDEA. Most courts use a version of "meaningful" or "significant" benefit, taking the child's ability level into account. However, the 11th Circuit Court of Appeals (governing federal courts in Florida, Georgia, and Alabama) has articulated and reaffirmed a far lower standard which essentially says that any progress is sufficient, even if the progress is not seen in any setting other than that in which the public agency claims it occurs (*J.S.K. v. Hendry Co. Sch. Bd.*, 1991). Difficult as this is for both special educators and parents to accept, it is the law in this one federal jurisdiction. The good news is that the huge majority of school personnel in every jurisdiction truly want to provide the best they can for every child who has a disability, without regard to what a federal appellate court has said. Nevertheless, parents in this one circuit must be especially careful to obtain thoroughly knowledgeable legal counsel before legally contesting an issue of 'how much progress is enough.'

When a Child is not Making Sufficient Progress

The first possible reason for inadequate progress that the IEP team should explore is that the services written into the IEP are not being delivered as promised. Difficult as this may be, both parents and school personnel need to explore this possibility candidly and aggressively. If the IEP team did its original job of determining needs, appropriate services and reasonably anticipated outcomes, then we assume these services will be appropriate. If not, a reasonable first question would be whether the services are actually happening as the team envisioned.

If the services are *not* being delivered as written in the IEP, the first strategy is two-fold: (a) insure the services *are* properly delivered beginning today, and (b) negotiate compensatory services to be delivered as soon as possible.

A common cause of children failing to make expected progress is that the *intensity* of services is not adequate, assuming that the services on the IEP are being delivered as written. Unfortunately, an increase in service is not always the easiest change to negotiate. If a requested increase in intensity is not provided, it is fully appropriate for parents to ask what change will be made and what the rationale is for believing that change will effectively improve the child's rate of progress.

In some circumstances a change in service provider might trigger greater progress for a child. However, that decision almost always rests with the LEA. The impact of the "highly qualified teacher" provision of NCLB may soon be felt in special education although related service providers may not be significantly affected. For now, parents may have to rely on the LEA's willingness to pursue a change in service providers.

When parents are convinced their child is not making appropriate progress and do not believe the proposed changes in service delivery or in the IEP, if any, will remedy the situation, they may consider obtaining private services or a private placement. We urge parents to procure good legal assistance before removing their child from the public placement. IDEA '04 has definite rules about what information parents must give the LEA and when the parents must provide it before a child is removed to private services. An error in how this is done can jeopardize the chances that the LEA will pay for private services or placement.

Mediation and alternative dispute resolution possibilities—less formal and legalistic than a due process hearing—may be available. Most of these alternate routes require voluntary participation by both parents and the LEA. In many LEAs school personnel refuse mediation on the advice of their attorneys, so a hearing may be the only option for parents.

Continuing Good Communication

Thank You Notes, Clarifying Phone Calls, Summary Letters

Very few serious disputes arise between school personnel and parents of children with disabilities as long as trust is high and communication open and clear. Keeping trust and communication intact is extremely important and never more so than when there has been a difficult IEP meeting or other differences have arisen.

School personnel deal with many parents and are not strangers to an occasional emotional meeting. Most are quite willing to overlook a lapse into less than positive messages. This is not to encourage such lapses, but to say they don't have to cause irreparable breaches. Professionals are not necessarily granted the same leeway. After a difficult meeting, both parents and professionals might consider writing a positive note or making a phone call, perhaps including a brief apology or acknowledgement of the difference that arose, stressing the value of agreements or common understandings that were reached, and committing to keeping the lines of communication and cooperation open. All parties should remember that the family and LEA will most likely have a long relationship and the more positive it is, the better for all concerned, especially the child.

Another positive contribution both the parents and school personnel can make to a good ongoing relationship is to minimize the time demands each makes, consistent of course with the needs and progress of the child. IDEA '04 encourages the combining of meetings (20 U.S.C. §1414 (d)(3)(E)) and allows alternative means of meeting participation such as video conferences and conference calls, if parents and school personnel agree.

Sometimes it seems as if all parties enter into the IEP process, that first IEP meeting, with an invisible bag of good will coins. If school personnel intimidate the parents, that "costs" the LEA a good will coin. If parents are too demanding, they lose a coin. If school personnel appear not to listen or hear, that costs a coin. If parents fail to stay on task during the meeting, another coin is lost. If the LEA fails to offer services sufficient to help the child progress, if the parents' advocate becomes abusive in the meeting . . . coins are lost. All parties must 'spend' their coins wisely. They must earn back additional coins if too many have been spent.

Earning back good will depends on genuinely conciliatory gestures being made and accepted. If the participants continue operating without any good will coins left, the situation can go from bad to worse to a due process hearing.

All IEP participants owe it to the other IEP team members, and most of all to the child, to keep some good will coins in reserve at all times. This may require an occasional gesture "above and beyond," an apology, a new found flexibility in service provision, a gift pack of herbal tea or other. Above all else, all team members must keep their focus on the child and providing what is appropriate for that child. Only by working together, maintaining a level of civility and good will, and constantly refocusing energy on how to address the child's needs, can all the team's resources be brought to bear on the child.

A suggestion that may seem superficial, but has been helpful for some teams, is to keep a large photograph of the child in the center of the IEP meeting table. At the first sign of interpersonal differences among team members, any member may say "Whoa, time out—our only real focus here is on Jake (pointing to photograph) and what his needs are and how we can address those needs." Refocus on the child, keep the focus on the child, and re-re-focus, as often as needed.

After all, the IEP meeting—the whole IEP process, IDEA itself—is all about the child's needs, the services to address the needs, and the goals (and progress markers) to evaluate the services so that the child receives a Free Appropriate Public Education.

> *A suggestion: Keep a large photograph of the child in the center of the IEP meeting table. At the first sign of interpersonal differences among team members, any member can say "time out—our only real focus here is on Jake (pointing to photograph).*

Discussing the Meeting with the Child

As important as parent-school relations are, the child has an even closer relationship to the school. An IEP meeting may result in changes to the child's schedule, routine, service providers or even placements. These may need to be discussed with the child, who may or may not have been at the meeting. For some children, such changes are not an issue; for others they may pose major issues. If school personnel and parents work together on planning and implementing the necessary steps, the child can be assisted to accept the changes or to at least be willing to try the new arrangements.

An Afterword

When all is said and done, a child's IEP can be a shining light showing the way, a year at a time, toward a brighter future. Or, sadly, it can be a meaningless formality, an utter waste of time and paper. Or somewhere in between. The usefulness of the IEP is largely in the hands of the IEP team, and is determined by the process of the IEP meeting.

Many IEPs, and more all the time, have made extremely valuable contributions to the education of millions of children who have disabilities. Every IEP can guide and improve the education of the child if the team focuses on identifying the child's needs (based on present levels of performance), providing the services to address those needs and objectively measuring progress toward the goal.

The only way we can know whether the services we provide are truly effective is by measuring the child's progress. If confronted by pressure to measure progress annually rather than quarterly or more often, IEP team members should assess carefully whether it is appropriate to provide ineffective services for a full year before learning we were on the wrong track. Clearly this cannot be in the child's interest.

> "…[A] school district [cannot] ignore the fact that an IEP is clearly failing, nor can it continue to implement year after year, without change, an IEP which fails to confer educational benefits on the student."(O'Toole v. Olathe District Schools Unified School District No. 233, 144 F. 3d 692 (10th Circuit 1998))

Perhaps we can all look forward to the time that FAPE truly means an effective program delivered by highly qualified teachers, as planned by an IEP team during pleasant and productive IEP meetings. When that day arrives, for every child who has a disability, the considerable promise of IDEA will have been delivered.

In conclusion, our hope is that no more IEPs ever need be found inadequate, as was one evaluated by a recent hearing review panel:

The IEP that was developed by the District was faulty and failed to properly address the student's deficiencies. It was not designed to enable the student to make meaningful educational progress, pursuant to Rowley. It did not provide the intensive program that the student needed for her 11th grade year, given her low and/or failing grades and severe disabilities. It provided for a "patch" or "band aid" instead of true remediation. In contrast to the District's argument, it certainly lacked transition planning for this student; lacked adequate tracking of the student's progress; and lacked specific direction as to what types of instructional approaches this student needs to develop her reading and math skills. (Bethlehem Sch. Dist., 41 IDELR 110, PA SEA 2004).

The parent's perspective on this same IEP process was also shared by the hearing review panel:

As the student's parent stated: "... it has [to] be in the IEP what the program is going to be, it has to define it, it has to give those goals and objectives and how they're going to track them because this is what—this is the tool we would have to hold the School District to the student's educational program. If it's not in the IEP they don't have to do it. And that's our understanding of how IEPs work. So there was a lot [of] vagueness in there that—and a lot of things that were said in the past on goals and objectives of the student, we didn't see them achieved or modified or happen in the past so it just seemed like a lot more of the same kind of system that we've had since middle school . . . It just seemed like more of the same kind of thing. It didn't seem like it was a description of a plan that was intense and going after the student's problems in a way that you could have followed it said that's going to—that's how this whole thing is going to work. It just seemed very open and vague. (Bethlehem Sch. Dist., 41 IDELR 110, PA SEA 2004).

Chapter 3

Appendix A & B

Writing Effective BIPs

We often assume that a child knows how to behave appropriately and is simply choosing inappropriate behaviors. This assumption is often false and never helpful. The team will do well to assume the child, in fact, needs to be taught the appropriate behaviors as well as when and how to employ them. In teaching a new behavior one of the critical elements is selecting the positive reinforcer for the desired, new behavior. Here is where parents have an extremely important contribution to make to the development of an effective BIP. They know better than anyone what things/activities/privileges are or could be truly meaningful positive reinforcers for the child. Well known behavioral psychologist, Phil McGraw, frequently observes that "*Every* child has a currency—something she or he will work hard to earn" (Casey & Cooper, 2004). We need to find and employ that currency, those consequences that are truly positive for each child. Individualization is a key mandate throughout all of IDEA 04 and nowhere is it more important than in planning the positive consequences in a BIP. No school official should ever be heard to say "*We* don't believe in positive rewards," or "*We* use the same reinforcers for all children" or "*We* use only a total group plan—if they all behave, they get a Friday treat." The task for the IEP team is to determine what consequences will be effective in changing *this* child's behavior.

Several criteria useful in examining the appropriateness of a BIP are "1) the BIP must be based on assessment data, 2) the BIP must be individualized to meet the child's unique needs, 3) the BIP must include positive behavior change strategies and 4) the BIP must be consistently implemented as planned and its effects monitored" (*Linn-Mar Community Sch. Dist. and Grant Wood Area Ed. Agency*, 41 IDELR 24 (Iowa SEA 2004)).

Since there is no prescribed form or format for a BIP, practice varies widely. The authors believe that the best BIP is as short and simple as it can be. It should be readily, quickly and completely understandable to all who should be using it— teacher, bus driver, playground assistant, cafeteria worker, vice principal or counselor. Consistency is one of the key ingredients in successful behavior changes. Therefore, a BIP should guide all those adults who have significant interactions with the child, especially in those environments or circumstances where the behaviors to be changed are likely to occur.

The IEP team might wish to employ the A-B-C model while developing a BIP. It is simple, but powerful and helpful. *A* stands for antecedents, the things that precede the behavior of concern. *A* can include the setting, what is happening and so on. In school situations, *A* is very often presenting the child with work or expectations beyond his present ability level. Another common antecedent (*A*) of inappropriate behavior is an unstructured situation such as recess or lunch time. *B* stands for the behavior of concern, the target behavior. Often, this is non-compliance, "shutting down" or acting out. *C* is for the consequence, what happens after the behavior. A simple but vital rule to understand is that when a behavior continues, the consequences are maintaining it. Every time Jake acts out in class, he is sent to the hall for 5 minutes. He keeps acting out. This tells us that sending him out of the room works well for him. That consequence is keeping the behavior going. It may also be true that excessively difficult work is the *A*, the antecedent that often triggers Jake's acting out. Changing the *A*, giving Jake only work within his present capability, is another way to affect the *B*, the behavior.

In short, to change Behavior, we must change the Antecedents and/or the Consequences. Typically, we must also teach the child how to do the desired, replacement behavior. The BIP should spell out, for all to see, how this is to happen.

One useful short BIP format, which is based on the A-B-C model (Bateman & Golly, 2003), answers these seven questions:

1. What are the child's strengths, interests, preferences? (these suggest possible positive reinforcers)

2. What are the problem behaviors? (stated specifically as behaviors, e.g., "curses at the teacher," rather than "is disrespectful")

3. What do we want him or her to do? (the desired behavior)

4. How will we teach the desired behavior? (a critical element, too often not included)

5. What can she or he earn by appropriate behavior? (the positive reinforcer)

6. What happens if she or he displays inappropriate behaviors? (the negative consequences)

7. How long will we try this plan? (rarely, if ever, longer than two weeks)

Basic Behavior Plan[23]

Name: _Nicolas_   Date: _____
Age: _9_   Grade: _4th_

What are his strengths?

Nicolas has great fine motor skills. He spends hours disassembling and assembling small mechanical objects (e.g., clocks, toy car engines, mixers). He loves tools and enjoys working on jigsaw puzzles. Nicolas has a great sense of humor and an infectious smile.

What are the problem behaviors?

Nicolas often refuses to stop an activity when asked. At first, he ignores the request. After several requests, when an adult removes the activity, Nicolas starts hitting the adult and screams that he wants to finish the project. The adults usually get him to calm down by promising that he will have an opportunity to finish the project later.

What do we want him to do?

Nicolas needs to follow directions the first time given. He needs to stop his "preferred" activity quickly and quietly and follow directions for the next activity.

How will we teach the desired behaviors?

An adult brainstorms a menu of reinforcers with Nicolas. After a list has been generated the adult explains to Nicolas that he/she wants to help him follow directions the first time given.

Role-play with Nicolas how to stop the "preferred" activity when asked by using examples and non-examples. First, let Nicolas be the "teacher." The adult pretends to be Nicolas and is working on a "preferred" activity. When Nicolas asks the adult to stop working on the engine and clean up, the adult will do it right the first time (example). Next, the adult mimics Nicolas' noncompliant behavior including the hitting and screaming (non-example). The last role-play will be a model of the expected behavior (example). After each role-play, Nicolas is asked if that was the right way and why.

After Nicolas is able to provide accurate feedback, roles will be reversed and Nicolas will be asked to stop the preferred activity. If he does it, he will receive lots of positive feedback and the adult will explain what he can earn if he can follow directions the first time given in class.

What can he earn?

Nicolas can earn pictures of tools (e.g., stickers). Each time he follows directions and stops a "preferred" activity, he can put a tool picture on a chart. When he has earned 10 "tools," his dad will get him a real toolbox. The next 10 stickers will earn him a real tool to put in his toolbox.

What happens if he displays unacceptable behaviors?

He will lose the opportunity to work on any preferred activity for the rest of the day.

How long will we try this plan?

The teacher will keep data. If Nicolas earns a sticker 8 out of 10 times the first week, the plan will be continued for 2 weeks. If Nicolas earns fewer than 5 stickers out of 10 times, a meeting to revise the plan will be called in one week.

---

[23]Developed by A. Golly and used with permission.

In some difficult situations, in order to develop an effective BIP, it may be necessary to find out more than is readily observable about the antecedents (As) and the maintaining consequences (Cs) for a child's behavior. More often the antecedents and consequences are fairly obvious. For example, every time his second grade reading group is asked to take turns reading aloud, Jimmy promptly begins teasing and hitting the children sitting next to him. He is then sent to the office for the duration of the reading lesson. About the second time this happens one might reasonably suppose that Jimmy prefers being in the office to reading aloud in his reading group. Another reasonable supposition is that his reading skills are inadequate and he doesn't want his peers to know. No further study is necessary beyond confirming that reading is difficult for Jimmy. The BIP can be developed as soon as Jimmy's positive reinforcers are identified.

In other situations, more and more careful observations may be required to fully understand the function the undesirable behavior serves for the child and this study is required by IDEA '04 in some discipline situations. The term "functional behavior assessment" (FBA) means a study of the behavior to learn its function for the child. Jimmy was acting inappropriately to avoid humiliation in front of his peers—the function of the behavior was to avoid something he didn't want to happen. Much inappropriate behavior serves the function of getting something the child does want, often adult or peer attention. The purpose of the FBA is to determine that function. This is done by studying records, by interviews, and by observing and then analyzing the situations in which the inappropriate behavior occurs and the consequences which maintain it.

Collecting these necessary data can be as simple as having a guided discussion with people who know the child and his or her behavior, or as demanding as doing repeated observations, formulating and testing hypotheses and doing more observations.

An FBA is usually done by school personnel and parents. In difficult, dangerous, or complex situations more expertise may be required. It may be necessary to set up situations in which the target behavior occurs and to then experimentally manipulate antecedents and consequences in order to determine how to change the behavior. This process is called functional analysis (FA) and should be done only by behavioral experts with specialized training.

If a child is removed from his or her current placement (for more than 10 days) for disciplinary reasons involving a weapon,[24] drugs or inflicting of serious bodily injury,[25] or if the disability did not cause the misconduct then the child shall "receive, *as appropriate*, a functional behavioral assessment, behavior intervention services and modifications, that are designed to address the behavior violation so that it does not recur" (20 U.S.C §1415 (k)(1)(D)(ii)).

If the offense did not involve a weapon, drugs or the infliction or serious bodily harm and it was caused by or substantially related to the disability, then the IEP team must conduct a functional behavioral assessment and a behavior intervention plan, if that has not already been done. If the child has a behavior intervention plan, it must be modified, as necessary (20 U.S.C. §1415 (k)(1)(F)(i, ii)).

A somewhat disconcerting, and hopefully short-lived trend is that some parents are now putting undue or misplaced hope and faith in FBAs. Too many parents seek to obtain an FBA as if it is always a vital part of every evaluation. Even in situations in which inappropriate behavior is not an issue, an FBA is being demanded by some. The hope is that it yields a "diagnosis" which will unlock the mystery of all the child's behavior, in a medical model framework. Parents and other IEP members need to be very clear about these basics of BIPs and FBAs:

---

[24] IDEA defines a weapon as a "dangerous weapon," which is a "weapon, device, instrument, material or substance, animate or inanimate that is used for or is readily capable of causing death or serious bodily injury. It does not include a pocket knife with a blade of less than 2½" in length" (18 U.S.C § 930 (g)(2)).

[25] (3) the term "serious bodily injury" means bodily injury which involves—

    (A) a substantial risk of death;
    (B) extreme physical pain;
    (C) protracted and obvious disfigurement; or
    (D) protracted loss or impairment of the function of a bodily member, organ, or mental faculty; and

(4) the term "bodily injury" means—

    (A) a cut, abrasion, bruise, burn, or disfigurement;
    (B) physical pain;
    (C) illness;
    (D) impairment of the function of a bodily member, organ, or mental function; or
    (E) any other injury to the body, no matter how temporary. (18 U.S.C. §1365 (h) (3,4))

1. A BIP is required by IDEA '04 when behavior is or may be problematic;

2. A BIP must include positive interventions;

3. The purpose of an FBA is to determine the function of the child's behavior, that is, what it is getting or avoiding for the child and what consequence (result) is maintaining the behavior;

4. The FBA may be so informal as to be nearly "invisible," or it may need to be formal, precise or elaborate, always depending on how difficult it is to determine the function of the behavior;

5. An FBA can contribute significantly to changing inappropriate behaviors; it is not necessary or even helpful when neither inappropriate behavior nor absence of appropriate behaviors is an issue;

6. The parents have highly valuable information to contribute to both BIPs and FBAs. This information often goes to the essential individualization of reinforcers, that is, what are truly positive and therefore effective consequences for their child; and

7. FBAs and BIPs are essential tools in the management of behavior and good practice requires us to employ them, regardless of legal mandates.

References

Bateman, B.D., & Golly, A. (2003). *Why Johnny doesn't behave: Twenty tips and Measurable BIPs*. Verona, WI: IEP Resources.

Brillion v. Klein Indep. School Dist., 41 IDELR 121 (5th Cir., 2004).

Casey, P., & Cooper, A. (Directors). (2004, September 21). *The Dr. Phil Show*. [Television broadcast]. Los Angeles: Harpo Productions.

Shaywitz, S. (2003). *Overcoming dyslexia: A new and complete science-based program for reading problems at any level*. New York: Alfred A. Knopf.

Family Rights and Privacy Act, 20 U.S.C. §1232g (1995).

J.S.K. v. Hendry Co. School Bd., 941 F. 2nd 1563 (11 Cir. 1991).

Tanner, L. (2004, November 11). Doctors are being encouraged to say they are sorry to avoid malpractice suits. *Associated Press Archive*. Retrieved January 22, 2005 from http://www.newslibrary.com.

Wright, P.W.D., & Wright, P. D. (2001) *From emotions to advocacy*. Hartfield, VA: Harbor House Law Press.

Wright, P.W.D., Wright, P.D., & Heath, S.W. (2003). *No child left behind*. Hartfield, VA: Harbor House Law Press.